Time & Time
Again

by Bob and Cheryl
Clarkson

Time and Time Again
by Bob and Cheryl Clarkson

ISBN: 0-9722278-1-4

14   13   12   11   10   6   5   4   3   2

Edited by Barbara Wooler and Viki Rife
Cover design by Laura Rife

The heart of man is filled with evil and desperately wicked. But there is not one heart that is so evil and wicked that it lies beyond the reach of the forgiveness and grace of God in Christ Jesus.

The story you are about to read is a true story of a man trapped in a vile world of evil, following the inclinations of a desperately wicked heart, hopelessly lost. This is also a story of the amazing grace of God and His strong love, complete forgiveness and continuing restoration. And this is a love story—love between brothers and sisters in Christ, and love between God and man—deep, lasting love, willing to take risks, weather the storms and take on and defeat the odds.

Many names in this story have been changed to protect the privacy of individuals, but the events are as true as memory and pen can tell.

Bob & Cheryl Clarkson
June 2002

Special Thanks...

... first and foremost to God, without whom my life transformation and this book telling that story, would never have happened.

... to Cheryl, my dedicated, Proverbs 31 wife.

... to our children, who gave us time alone to write this book, and are the greatest children any father could want.

... to Elizabethtown and Hope Grace Brethren Churches for their encouragement, love and faithful support through the years.

... to Chaplain Wilson, my mentor while I was in prison, and the one who encouraged me to write my story.

... to Pastor George Traub of the Hope Grace Brethren Church (Dillsburg, PA) for his encouragement, love and faithful mentoring through the years.

... to Officer Hoffman, for showing me care and compassion.

... to Ray Melvin, for discipling me and for his friendship.

... to Mom & Dad Tweeddale for their prayers and support.

... to Mom and Dad Clarkson and my family, for always being there whether I was good or bad.

... to James and Cherie Brown and Jason, for all the time they spent on the computer.

... to our dear fellow-warrior in the Lord, Barb Wooler, and to all those who typed, edited and proofread so that this book could happen.

... to Pastor Herritt for his deliverance ministry.

... to CE National for making the publishing of this book a reality.

... and to the Fellowship of Grace Brethren Churches, for its love for the Lord and commitment to keeping the Gospel pure.

Bob Clarkson

June 2002

Table of Contents

Part I: On the Wrong Side of the Cross

Part II: Turning to Christ and Into a Disciple

Part III: Grace House

Part I:
Life on the Wrong Side
of the Cross

Not Again!

The bars clanged shut. "Not again!" Every fiber of RC's heart was exploding with the words. He slammed the bars with his hands in anger, defiance and pain. He turned to his life-long friend, Scotty, who had just been locked up with him. "I can't believe I'm in here again!" he said. "I've only been out two weeks!"

"RC, I ain't been in jail for years. I never expected we'd get caught."

"Scotty, I'll be sitting in here a long time. Nobody's going to put up bail for me—no one will get me out of here this time." In his heart he knew that no one would work to get him out. He could not rely on Susan, his girlfriend, even though she was holding thousands of dollars in money orders he'd recently stolen. She would use this time to enjoy her freedom: freedom from the pain he'd caused her, freedom from his drunkenness and the violent man he became when drunk, freedom from the explosive anger and hostility that erupted from bitterness and pain buried deep within his soul, freedom from his control and the physical and emo-

Attempting to take his life again looked appealing. A quick snap of his neck at the end of a rope and it would all be over.

tional abuse that always followed the anger. Yes, she would let him sit. There was no point in even wasting his thoughts on Susan or the money she had available to get him out.

His frustration mounted into despair. How he hated jail! How he hated life! RC eyed the showerhead at the end of the dorm room shared with so many other inmates. Attempting to take his life again looked appealing. A quick snap of his neck at the end of a rope and it would all be over. This stinking, pain-filled life would be over and he would be done with it. It just wasn't worth living anymore. He lay on the bunk that night, insomnia again consuming him. As he listened to the snoring of men just inches from his bunk on both sides, his thoughts again took him back to pain-filled memories, like a lousy rerun with no "off" button.

A Rough Start

On November 2, 1958, Roberta and Francis Dougherty brought a little boy into the world. Robert Francis Dougherty, named after his mother and father, was born around 1:30 p.m. at the Temple Hospital in Philadelphia.

To understand RC's troubled life, one must consider first the troubled life of his biological mother, Roberta. Roberta and her brother had been taken by the Children's Aid Society when they were still very young because they were being neglected. Agnes and Harry Clarkson, who could have no children of their own, adopted the two children.

Roberta's adopted mother, Agnes, had been raised very properly in the home of Newton and Agnes Challenger. This home was a strict one. During the early 1900's the Kensington section of Philadelphia was filled with knitting mills, and from an early age Agnes worked on the looms. She soon became an expert seamstress. While Roberta and Billy were growing up, Agnes spent many hours sewing all of their clothes. She and Harry raised eleven children during their lifetime, none of them their own. The children were taken faithfully to the United Methodist Church and raised properly and strictly.

From a young age, Roberta rebelled. As a young woman she ran off and married Francis Dougherty, an abusive man with a drinking problem who committed crimes of theft. Their rocky marriage produced four children: Frances, Henry, Robert (RC), and Billy. Roberta finally had enough. She left Francis, dropping her children off with her adoptive parents, Agnes and Harry, for them to raise.

RC was about two years old when he came to live with his grandparents. Agnes and Harry later adopted all four children, changing their name from Dougherty to Clarkson.

Robert Frances Dougherty was around seven at the time of

his adoption. He asked to change his middle name also. Even at this young age he had a great deal of bitterness, anger and pain in his heart toward his parents for pushing him out of their lives. He resolved to change Francis (after his father) to James, after his best friend in school at that time. His legal name became Robert James Clarkson. RC would be nine before he'd see his biological mother again; and neither his father nor his mother ever returned to visit RC.

In terms of the religious training of the children, Agnes Clarkson was on her own. Though Harry was a Catholic, he rarely attended church and took no part in the children's religious training. So Agnes did what she could. Her theology concerning salvation was at best confused, and in an attempt to put the fear of God in young RC's heart, she repeatedly told him that he would never make it into Heaven. RC took these words to heart, but instead of fearing God more and doing what was right, he figured he might as well be as bad as he wanted to be, since he would never make it to Heaven anyway.

The parenting skills of his grandparents were not perfect, of course. They were both quick to lose their temper and could overdo it on discipline. Both had great difficulty expressing any words of love or affection. Still, each of the children knew they were loved by their adoptive parents. Every summer Agnes and Harry planned a big vacation to Atlantic City for all the children. They would spend a whole week taking the children on the rides and to the beach, and they would treat them to delicious foods on the boardwalk. Sometime during each year they also planned a special family trip to a resort or amusement park. The kids looked forward to these times and enjoyed many adventures at such places as Santa Claus Land, Frontier Land, Dutch Wonderland and Niagara Falls.

Agnes and Harry tried their best to replace the parents RC had lost. Still, RC could not get over the hurt of having been deserted and rejected by his biological parents. The fact that he was adopted was kept painfully in front of him during his school years as he endured the tormenting of other children, who would at times tease him mercilessly about being adopted. This teasing made him even more angry, and he began lashing out in anger at anyone who got in his way. He expressed this

14

anger not only in violent ways, but also through devious and destructive behavior. During these early years he not only stole from others and was drawn into many fights, but soon he began to be the one starting the fights.

RC's grandmother remembers an incident where she was called to school to come and get her son, RC, who was in the second grade at the time. When she arrived at the school she was taken quickly to the classroom, where the desks, children and teacher were all pushed into a corner. RC was standing in the middle of the classroom with a chair raised in his hands, screaming at the shaken class.

The incident had started when some of the kids were picking on RC about being adopted. Someone hit him in the back of the head, and the teacher blamed him for the disturbance. This triggered his explosive anger. He began shoving the desks, children and teacher into a corner.

His grandmother calmed him down and took him home. There his grandfather, who rarely got involved in the punishment of the children, gave him a good spanking.

It is important to remember that the generation of children growing up in the fifties and sixties rarely knew anyone from a broken home. Divorce, desertion, and adoption were almost

RC was standing in the middle of the classroom with a chair raised in his hands, screaming at the shaken class.

unheard of among the school children during this time. So there was always a stigma attached to RC because his parents had abandoned him and were divorced, and because RC was adopted. Kids can be cruel, and RC, due to the circumstances of his life, became a target for their cruelty.

RC's explosive anger was a continual part of his life. It was like a time bomb that went off inside his head any time he was blamed for anything he did or did not do. It erupted like a volcano from the center of his being, spraying anyone and everyone involved with its destructive heat. The recipients, often caught completely off guard, were left shaken and confused.

This incident in the classroom was the first of many episodes of violent anger displayed publicly by RC. It was his desperate attempt to get the children in his classroom to back off and not to pick on him about circumstances of his life over which he had no control. These conflicts, caused by the combination of the children's cruel comments and RC's sensitivity, pain and anger, taught him at an early age to fight. Often he was beaten up, but as he grew older, stronger and more educated in street fighting, he soon gained a reputation to be respected.

When RC was about nine, he overheard his grandmother telling his grandfather that Roberta, RC's biological mother, had just bought a house on Raymond Street in Philadelphia. RC listened carefully from the next room as they described where the house was located. He longed to see his mother, whom he only knew from pictures. He longed for his mother to hug him— to tell him she was sorry and that she loved him.

The next day he took a bus, then walked the rest of the distance to his mother's house. Scared and shaking inside, he walked up the steps and knocked on the door.

After what seemed like an eternity, Roberta answered the door. She looked down, recognized young RC, and greeted him harshly. "What are you doing here?" she growled. His heart dropped.

How could she give him up, then have more kids? How could she not want anything to do with him?

He looked behind her into the house and saw several children. "Who are those kids?" he asked. "They are your brother and sisters," she replied.

When she refused to let him in, he turned and left, confused and heartbroken. An overwhelming sense of emptiness settled in.

He cried as he walked all the way home. How could she give him up, then have more kids? How could she not want anything to do with him? Hurt turned to anger, and anger to rage and hatred.

That evening he vented his mounting anger by setting his first of many fires, burning a carpet mill on Allegheny Avenue.

He tried several more times, mostly out of curiosity, to see his mother and other siblings, but he was never welcome. Questions filled his mind. Why was he unwanted? What was wrong with him? How could she just have new kids by another man?

Finally, RC realized there was no hope for reconciliation with his mother. His efforts to visit stopped. He could not take the pain anymore.

He did not see her again until he finished high school.

Turning To Crime

RC's adoptive parents were extremely worried about RC's bent towards crime. At the age of five, RC stole gum while with his grandmother. She did not discover the gum on him until they had reached home. Immediately she called the police. When they arrived she pulled them aside, explained what happened, and asked them to help teach RC a lesson. Soon RC was in the police car being escorted to the police station. They locked him up for ten minutes!

This incident frightened RC, but it did not cure him of stealing. It was as though he were driven to commit crime after crime.

When RC was seven, his grandmother, frustrated and distraught over yet another incident of stealing, disciplined RC by putting his hands over a lit burner to "teach him a lesson." Although again very frightened by this punishment, the lesson RC learned was to make sure he did not get caught the next time.

When RC was nine, he and a next-door neighbor boy broke into a boy's club called Lighthouse Field. They stole all the baseball equipment they could carry. RC wanted to play pinball—something his grandmother forbade him to play, but which he loved with a passion. Since he only received a dime a week for his allowance, he needed more money to play pinball. This crime would provide the money he needed for his pinball "habit." So RC and his friend began selling the baseball equipment in the neighborhood.

Within four days the Juvenile Aid Division came to his door and took him to the police station, charging him and his friend with the crime. His grandparents came and got him and took him home. A few days later he went to his first court hearing, where his grandmother testified to his out-of-control behavior. The judge ordered him to the Youth Study Center (YSC), a juvenile detention facility. RC spent four days at the YSC. While there, he was evaluated psychologically and diagnosed with multiple problems.

On his release, he was sentenced to four years of intensive psychiatric probation. Every ten days his grandmother had to take him to a psychiatrist, where he was diagnosed as a paranoid schizophrenic and a kleptomaniac with pyromaniac tendencies. Three times a month he was seen by his P.O. (probation officer). This regimen continued for three years, with RC's behavior spiraling more and more out of control.

Agnes and Harry, frustrated and at a loss as to what to do with RC, repeatedly reported his behavior to the P.O. The P.O. in turn began to threaten RC with being placed again in the YSC. So, at the age of twelve, RC ran away from home for the first time. A friend of RC's from the neighborhood knew an old drunk who would let them stay with him.

While living with this drunk, RC's stealing grew to greater proportions. There were several other runaways living with the drunk, as well. As long as the boys supplied the drunk with beer, they had a home.

Living here among these other boys, RC gained a greater education in stealing and burglary. RC lived with this man until he was fourteen. Finally, after a string of burglaries, he was caught, convicted and sentenced to two years in St. Gabriel's Hall.

St. Gabriel's Hall was a boarding school for court-sentenced delinquent boys. During his stay at St. Gabriel's, RC ran away fourteen times. The school was run by very strict Franciscan brothers who wore long, black robes. RC could not tolerate the restrictive, disciplined environment and longed to be on his own again.

Although he rebelled against the discipline, he remembers fondly two house parents, Brother Paul and Brother Barry, who encouraged him to do right, told him he could be somebody, looked after him and really cared for him. When he would run away, they would be there when he was taken back, encouraging him and loving him. It was one of the few times in his life when he felt accepted and cared for.

While at St. Gabriel's RC learned useful skills such as woodworking, leather craft and making pottery. But unfortunately, while there he also continued to increase his knowledge of criminal ways as he listened to the boastful adventures of the other budding criminals. Even though the school was well respected as a facility for reforming delinquent boys, it was also a hothouse for learning all kinds of evil. Here the boys would share stories of how to steal cars and credit cards, how to burglarize houses and stores, and commit various other crimes which had landed them at St. Gabriel's.

Sunday was a day of religious training for everyone, but unfortunately the gospel was not part of the boys' training. Communion was given for those who wanted to partake, and RC usually did. As the priest handed the wafer to RC he would offer these

RC would go away from these communion times feeling a little relieved inside, but he always found he had no inner restraint to keep him from doing wrong.

words, "You are forgiven, my son." RC would go away from these communion times feeling a little relieved inside. For a while he would attempt to improve his behavior, but he always found that for the rest of the week he still had no inner restraint to keep him from doing wrong. The only inner impulse he felt was the persistent emptiness that always plagued him. The thrill and excitement of criminal activity was the only thing he had found to help him forget, if only for a short time, the gnawing emptiness that ate away at his soul.

All the while he was haunted by fear, recalling his grandmother's words, "Bobby, you will never be good enough to get into Heaven."

Drugs and alcohol played an important role in RC's life, dulling the feelings of emptiness. Even while in St. Gabriel's, he was able to get his hands on substances to help him numb the aching pain of his soul. At a very young age, while RC still lived at home, he and his best friend Chas had experimented with sniffing glue, smoking pot and drinking. As he grew older, he found himself returning to use these substances more and more. Several times when he escaped from St. Gabriel's as a young teenager, his purpose for escaping was to acquire drugs and alcohol.

At sixteen RC was kicked out of St. Gabriel's. He had just run away again, and when he was apprehended, the authorities at St. Gabriel's told him to pack his bags. They were giving him no more chances. They drove him home and placed him again in the care of his grandparents. Agnes and Harry enrolled him at Edison High in Philadelphia. It was one of the roughest schools in Philadelphia at the time, and RC began to get into fights with the other students from the start.

Shortly after his return home, money that Agnes and Harry had been saving in a lock box in their home disappeared. Immediately Agnes fingered RC with the theft and ordered him out of the house. Angrily, bitterly, he packed his bags. This time he was innocent! Much later, his brother finally admitted guilt for the crime.

After leaving home, RC lived here and there with friends. Eventually the authorities caught up with him for probation violations. They placed him back at the YDC (Youth Detention Center) in Cornwall Heights, in the maximum-security section for juvenile offenders. He remained there for almost a year. One good thing came from it: during that time he was able to graduate from high school.

The YDC officials invited his mother Roberta, as well as his adopted mother Agnes, to his graduation. He was graduating with honors, and they hoped to help heal some of his hurt by inviting his biological mother. Surprisingly, Roberta came to RC's graduation. The officials asked her to come to a side room for the initial private meeting. RC had not seen his mother since long ago when she had turned him away at her door. He was unaware that his mother had been invited to the graduation. When RC entered the room and saw her, his heart swelled with rage, and he lashed out at his mother, shouting, "What are you doing here?" The guards called a special counselor, Lou, because of RC's explosion and emotional unsettledness. Lou calmed him down. Roberta stayed in a separate room for the duration of the service, while Agnes joined RC in the festivities.

RC would never see his mother again. Within a few years, at the age of forty-one, she would die of a sudden brain hemorrhage.

RC had several months left until he turned eighteen. Tired of being locked up and away from his friends and family, he got a friend to sneak him a chisel, which he used to break out through the window and escape. As he attempted to climb over a double barbed wire fence, the barbs caught him in the groin area and ripped a big hole in his body.

He made it over and caught a bus to his friend Butchy's house. Butchy's mother, a nurse, patched him up and let him stay there while he healed.

After several months, he was again apprehended by the police and placed in the Youth Study Center to await his hearing. The judge released him with the warning that he would soon be eighteen, and if he messed up he would be tried as an adult.

He got a friend to sneak him a chisel, which he used to break out through the window and escape.

When he was released he moved in with some friends. One day his brother invited him to a party. Many of his old friends were going to be there, so RC went along. At the party, RC met Susan, a woman several years older than him. She had four young children by previous relationships. Knowing he needed a place to live, she invited him to stay with her. This was the beginning of a seven-year, on-again-off-again relationship.

RC and Susan's home became a hangout, attracting many of RC's old friends with whom he had grown up and done time at the YDC or at various other places. Like magnets,

23

they were drawn to each other by their common interests in crime and their continual need for drugs, sex, alcohol and money. Using the knowledge he acquired about crime in the YDC and at various other places, RC began to commit crime after crime. Committing a robbery or burglary gave RC a high. It was thrilling and euphoric, giving him a feeling of well-being, security and power as he brought home stacks of money or jewelry.

RC and his old friends began to organize their waves of crime throughout the city. Their days were spent organizing, plotting and scheming their next event, when they would rob or burglarize another victim, establishment or home. For over a year RC managed to evade being caught. But finally he was apprehended for a burglary and given four years probation. Not wanting to answer to anyone, he jumped parole and fled to New Jersey to live with his brother, who helped him get a job as a guard in one of the casinos.

RC was able to use his position as a guard to steal from various local businesses and amusement centers. He stayed in New Jersey for a few months until his brother joined the army. During those months RC would make periodic trips back to Philadelphia to repair his relationship with Susan. Susan moved to a house on Front Street, making it possible for RC to come back home, since the parole officers no longer knew where he lived.

RC and Susan had a rocky relationship from the start. RC's drinking and drug problem was out of control. He found himself reaching throughout the day for speed and alcohol. The speed helped him stay awake when he was tired from his nightly escapades and gave him a rush of euphoria. The alcohol he used to calm himself down from the speed. The two drugs always went together. The drinking and drug problem was out of control.

Rarely sober, RC was incapable of maintaining a secure, loving relationship. The arguing and fighting escalated into explosive outbursts, often resulting in abuse. The abuse drove Susan out of their home, and she would find temporary shelter with friends. Coming to his senses later, RC would search for her, truly sorry for his behavior, and would win her back.

During this time, Susan became pregnant with RC's first child, her fifth. Together they had been raising her four other children by previous relationships. RC held on to a small hope that this baby would help bring about a change in his life, providing the motivation he needed to get a job and live straight. He soon realized that this was not the case.

Robert William Clarkson was born on May 24, 1978. RC was overcome at the sight of his beautiful baby boy. He was totally blown away by the wonder of his son. Almost immediately, though, his thoughts turned from little Bobby and all the joy he brought, to the question of how his own mother could have given him away when he was a child. These thoughts opened the festering wounds even further. RC's heart hardened in pain, and his behavior went from bad to worse.

Disillusioned, realizing that even fatherhood could not change his heart, he remained bent more than ever on doing wrong and destroying whatever got in his way, drowning his pain in escalating drug and alcohol abuse.

RC held on to a small hope that this baby would help bring about a change in his life, providing the motivation he needed.

Little Bobby was about a year old when RC's brother-in-law came knocking on their door. He was frantic and excited as he asked for RC's help. Two of their old friends had just escaped from an armed police car and needed help getting out of their handcuffs. RC went to the house and removed the cuffs. Little did he know that this meeting would forever change his heart and the way he looked at life and death.

Together the four men planned a robbery they felt was a sure thing, enabling them to secure thousands of dollars from a locked safe. After two days of planning the robbery, they set the time for 6 a.m. the next morning. At 2 a.m. RC went to his house for some sleep. He was cold from lack of heat in the house, tired from being up for so many days, and very sick and nauseated from doing too many drugs.

RC overslept. He was awakened from his sleep by a lot of commotion outside. Police cars were arriving; the officers were investigating a murder. RC, shaken and confused, went over to his brother-in-law's to find out what had happened. When he realized that the plan had resulted in a murder, RC was deeply shaken. He saw God in his mind's eye staring at him from above, full of wrath. Deep within his heart he knew, he just knew, that now God would never accept him, under any conditions, into Heaven. To make matters worse, the store-keeper who had been murdered was a man who had been kind and good to RC since he was a young boy.

The reality of all of this, the pain and torment of it all, made him give up inside. Feelings of hopelessness, emptiness and loss stormed his heart. Maybe he was just put on this earth to steal and rob and do wrong, and then die and go to Hell. Was this his lot? He was tormented with thoughts of the anger of God, eternity in Hell, never being good enough, never measuring up. RC gave up inside. He would not even try any more to achieve any level of acceptance with God. He knew it was useless. He was a hopeless cause. His grandmother was right. He would never amount to any good.

When he realized that the plan had resulted in murder, RC was deeply shaken. He just knew that now God would never accept him.

This change in his thinking, this hardness of heart and despair, opened his heart to an even more destructive, futile path. Now, with the twisted thinking that eternity in Hell was his lot, RC, more depraved in mind and heart, robbed the storekeeper's shop while the funeral proceedings were taking place, cleaning out the store over the next four days through a hole in the roof. Thousands of dollars in money and supplies stolen from the store provided enough for several weeks of non-stop partying, drinking and drugs.

It was a few weeks later that the police came to RC's door and told him he was under arrest for a string of burglaries. Feigning innocence, he told them he didn't know what they were talking about. Little did he know that a friend of his, who had been apprehended and was out in the police car, had given them his name.

RC was convicted and sentenced to the detention center on State Road, where he spent several months. It was there that he first began in earnest to seek answers in the religious services. He hoped that possibly Agnes had been wrong, that maybe there was a chance for him to find acceptance with God. He heard a lot of singing, praying and messages, but never heard the gospel presented—never heard of the forgiveness of sin offered through Jesus Christ.

During the months RC spent in the detention center he heard nothing from Susan. So after his release he went looking for her. When he found her, they moved into the house on Mascher Street where RC had been raised as a child. It had been sitting boarded up, and RC just moved in. His grandmother, found out he was living there and said it was okay, as long as he paid $100 rent each month. She never received a penny of this rent—RC and Susan never paid rent or bills in any of their homes. They would live in a place until evicted, then move on to another place.

They lived on Mascher Street several months. During that time Susan became pregnant with their second child. RC soon found himself arrested for another set of burglaries and was sent back to the detention center. His brother bailed him out this time and his grandmother came to the detention center and brought him home to live with her for a while in Norristown. While he was living there his grandmother went out, got little Bobby Clarkson from Susan's, and brought him to live with them. Later, when RC's second child, little Joanne, was born, he went to Susan's house, took her from her crib, and brought her to live with them as well.

In Norristown, at the age of twenty-three, while living with his grandmother he began working his first real job as a sexton in the United Methodist Church that Agnes attended. Lying to his grandmother and hanging out at the bars, he soon met up with bad company and began to burglarize again, stealing now even from the church he was working for. Soon he was caught again and sent back to the detention center on State Road.

Agnes worked hard to get RC out this time, being deceived by his lies into believing that he was making an effort to do right and live straight. RC did indeed want to do what was right, which was why he had taken the job as a sexton in the first place, but he just seemed powerless to hold himself to doing what was right.

When he was out, he began to work for Dunkin Donuts. There he met Dana, who worked with him on the night shift. Here RC met up with many other drug addicts and drinkers, and began to drink heavily every day, with the drinking always leading to drug abuse. Working the eleven to seven shift provided a lack of supervision, and cases of beer and drugs would be brought to work each night. Getting high was what RC lived for each day.

Working the eleven to seven shift provided a lack of supervision, and cases of beer and drugs would be brought to work each night.

Eventually, RC and Dana got married and rented a little place. New management replaced the night crew of Dunkin Donuts, and RC lost his job. Once again he began to burglarize for his livelihood. During this time Agnes moved to New Jersey to be closer to Franny, RC's sister. RC sent Little Bobby and Joanne to live with their grandmother, not wanting them to be hurt by his out-of-control living, the drinking and the drugs.

After a big fight one day, Dana left RC and took off for Nevada to live with her dad for a while. RC, finding himself alone, went to New Jersey to live with his grandmother and children. He was weary of the life he was living and wanted his family back.

He began attending Alcoholics Anonymous/Narcotics Anonymous in a little garage in Gloucester City, N.J., owned by a man named Gary. This group disputed the validity of the

Bible. They believed that what was taught in most churches was misleading and would cause greater confusion, so members were warned not to attend. RC stuck with this group for several months, religiously attending meetings several times each week. Gary even gave him a job, training him to be an ironworker and sheet metal mechanic building gas stations. With things looking up, Dana returned to live with RC, his grandmother and the kids.

Years of Searching

The fourth step in the twelve-step program at AA/NA instructed RC to look to a higher power for aid in overcoming his addiction. His sponsor, Ken, an atheist, claimed a vase as his higher power, and ran to the vase for help and strength when weak. RC, feeling things were working for Ken, also adopted the vase as his higher power, but even as he ran to his "higher power" for help and strength, he felt continuing emptiness and loss.

One night, after a big fight, RC relapsed back into drinking and drugs. He continued attending some of the AA meetings, finding acceptance even in his relapsed condition, being taught that ultimately he was powerless to overcome his addiction. Off and on over the next ten years RC continued to reach out for help through these programs. But he was becoming increasingly disillusioned and frustrated, overwhelmed by a feeling of hopelessness.

RC continued working for Gary off and on over the next seven years. They developed a good friendship, and Gary was always willing to hire RC back after he had served time in jail for different sentences. RC had become a skilled sheet metal mechanic, and Gary valued his work. Even though his job was very lucrative, RC continued to burglarize on occasion. The thrill of robbing and stealing continued to be a way of filling the deep emptiness RC felt with life and the unhealed pain of his past.

Dana stuck with RC, in spite of the rockiness of their relationship. In 1985, they had a beautiful little girl and named her Christine, after Dana's mother.

Around 1988 RC was again locked up for burglary. This time he was placed in the Montgomery County Jail in Norristown. During these months in jail, Dana and RC lost their house in

New Jersey, so when RC was released they moved back to Kensington, Philadelphia.

RC became haunted every day by the things he had done that he was not proud of. Trying to numb the pain and fill the void, he would start the day with drinking. Purchasing a case of beer a day, he would work on a couple beers in the morning and soon feel on top of the world. Then he would head over to a friend's house and do some drugs. Needing money to continue his binge, he would go out with a friend looking for someone to rob, an unlocked car, an open window somewhere—any way to steal something that they could then sell to a grocer on the avenue, who would buy their merchandise for a small price.

With their money, they bought more drugs—a $3 bag of crack, a $10 bag of cocaine, and a $10 bag of heroin. When the money ran out they were out on the streets again, and again, and again. They would go on a run for days, until their bodies were completely exhausted from lack of sleep and little food. They would then go home and literally pass out for twenty-four hours, only to get up and do it all again. RC was trapped in this world. Trapped! At times he felt deep despair and loss. Sometimes he even cried out, because he had tried every way to get out of this life of hell. Nothing was working.

RC had been out of jail only a few short weeks, with the drinking, drugs and crime completely out of control, when he was once again arrested for a string of burglaries that had taken place in his neighborhood. Although he had participated in some of the burglaries, he had not been out of jail long enough to be involved in the whole string of burglaries for which he was being tried. With his time in jail as an alibi, he was released by the court.

The business community was upset by RC's release. He soon found himself hunted by some men who were paid to do him harm. Realizing his danger, RC and Dana moved back to Norristown.

Shortly after moving back, in January of 1990, RC became violently sick with intestinal pain and cramping. He went to a clinic in Norristown. A number of tests failed to find the source of the pain. Finally they tested him for HIV.

The test came back positive. The doctor counseling RC told him with concern that he felt they might be able to keep him alive for five years.

The news completely devastated RC's world. He was convinced that there was no reason to live any longer. Shocked and confused, he got high again, going on a long drug run and burglarizing to get the money to obtain drugs, the only thing he had found to numb the pain.

They tested him for HIV. The test came back positive.

Then one day the police came to his house. RC realized that they were coming to arrest him for a burglary. He went out to meet them swinging a bicycle by the handle bars. He screamed for the police to just shoot him, kill him, put him out of his misery! Somehow they subdued him and took him to Montgomery County Prison. Angry and afraid, he tried to hang himself. A guard came by just in time and cut him down. He couldn't even succeed at dying!

As he sat in jail, he learned that Dana had moved in with another man. RC was completely devastated. In one fast swoop his whole world was again knocked out from under him. Unable to disclose his illness in jail, he kept everything bottled up inside—pain, remorse, and despair.

Once again he began to attend church services in jail, trying to find a source of comfort and consolation. Deep down he felt there had to be answers. He even talked to the priest, but found nothing to ease his pain and despair.

When he finally got out of jail, RC looked up Gary again. Gary gave him back his old job building gas stations and helped him find a place to live..

But RC kept finding himself getting sick at work. Gary questioned him and RC was at a loss what to tell him. Becoming confused, he began drinking, finally working up the courage to tell Gary the truth. Gary, frightened by RC's disclosure, decided to lay RC off.

Without family or job, sick with HIV, RC began drinking and doing drugs non-stop. One day he called his friend, Mark, and they began planning to rob a neighborhood bar. However, instead of doing what they had planned, Mark panicked and took off when the bag of money was in RC's hand. Soon RC had two men chasing him.

Attempting to escape, RC jumped a fence. As he was going over the top, part of the fence caught his knee. Unable to move his leg, he was quickly apprehended. After a trip to the hospital, where his knee was stitched up, he was taken to Camden County Jail Medical Department. There he was placed on the AIDS block, segregated from the general prison population. The AIDS block was cold. The inmates on the AIDS block slept on thin mattresses on the floor. The guards made ill-humored remarks about these sick inmates. Often RC found his medications withheld, or his food was brought to him cold.

As sickness engulfed him, he was sure this was where he was going to die. Lying on the cold floor at night, he became consumed in his heart with taking revenge for the way they were being treated. He and others on the AIDS block started working on a lawsuit against the administration.

Meanwhile, in his desperation, he reached out for help to his old AA/NA support group. A couple of members came to visit him. Shortly after their visit, RC received a letter—a very unusual letter.

The Letter

RC's daughter, Joanne, along with Susan's other four girls, had been taken from her mother and sent to live in the foster home of Cheryl Tweeddale. One evening Cheryl received a phone call from Agnes Clarkson. Agnes informed them that Joanne's father, RC, was in the Camden County Jail. She also let them know of her concern for RC's health—he was dying of AIDS.

Cheryl wrote down RC's address and hung up the phone. She was overcome with grief and concern. Cheryl had come to love little Joanne like her own daughter. As a Christian, Cheryl longed for the permanent healing only Jesus Christ could bring to the lives of her children and their biological parents. To think of RC dying in that miserable cell without ever knowing of the love and forgiveness of Christ, then spending an eternity in Hell, separated from God, was more sorrow than she could bear.

After the children were in bed, Cheryl began to write RC a letter. It went something like this.

"Dear RC,

Hi, my name is Cheryl Tweeddale. I am the foster mother of your daughter Joanne. Your mother called this evening and told us of your predicament of being in jail and having the AIDS virus. Please allow me to speak openly and from the heart. RC, every one of us is a sinner, separated from God's love because of our sin. The Bible puts it like this, *"For all have sinned and fall short of the glory of God."* Romans 3:23. Because God loved us and created us for Himself, He desired to once and for all restore our relationship with Himself which was destroyed in the Garden of Eden when Adam and Eve sinned. So, out of His great love He sent His own Son Jesus Christ to die on the cross to pay for our sins. We all deserved death, but instead Jesus went to the cross in our place. He alone is perfect, so God could accept His Son's death in place of all mankind.

The Bible also says *"If we confess our sin He is faithful and just and will forgive us our sin and cleanse us from all unrighteousness"* (I John 1:9) and *"If thou shalt confess with thy mouth the Lord Jesus and believe in thine heart that God hath raised Him (Jesus) from the dead thou shalt be saved"* (Romans 10:9).

"Please, RC, read these verses carefully and consider what God has said. No matter what anyone has done, God will forgive him through the blood of His Son, Jesus Christ."

"RC, we must confess our sin, believe God's Word, and receive Jesus Christ into our lives, accepting His payment of death on the cross in our place. When we do this, we are justified (made clean) by faith in Jesus Christ. God pronounces us "not guilty." We become God's own children, just as it says in John 1:12, *"To all who received him, to those who believed in his name, he gave the right to become children of God,"* and He promises that when His children die He will take us to Heaven.

Please, RC, read these verses carefully and consider what God has said. No matter what anyone has done, God will forgive him through the blood of His Son, Jesus Christ. I will be praying for you. We love you and will be in touch. Maybe we can come for a visit.

Love,

Cheryl

At RC's request, the AA/NA members came for a second visit. He began telling them of the unusual letter he had received. With concern, they strictly told him not to listen to what Cheryl had to say, that this would only confuse him and lead him down a path headed nowhere.

RC was tormented in his thoughts. He had gone after AA/NA with gusto. He had devoted himself to the twelve steps system and its principles, but still he kept falling, kept slipping. If something were real and true, wouldn't it have the power to keep him from falling? Wasn't there some hope, something to rescue him from the enemy within himself?

He read Cheryl's letter over and over. He picked up the Bible and read it, then put it down, not knowing if what he was doing would help. Maybe his friends were right. Maybe this was all taking him down a path leading nowhere. He read Cheryl's letter again and again.

Eight and a half months later, he was taken to trial. He was sentenced to seven years in the State Penitentiary.

At Southern State, RC faithfully attended the AA/NA classes. He was desperate to change the life he had screwed up so badly. Still confused, he also began attending church every Sunday. He continued to correspond with Cheryl and began to re-establish his relationship with Joanne and Rob, his son, who was now also living with Cheryl.

In his letters to Cheryl, so as not to offend, he wrote frequently of his faith in God and Jesus Christ, but inwardly he was still very confused. Many individuals from his AA/NA meetings were discouraging him from reading the Bible or placing his faith in Jesus Christ. He was hesitant to place his faith in someone he was so unsure of.

One day Cheryl came to the prison to bring RC's children to visit. RC was glad to see his children. He was also struck by the peace that Cheryl seemed to have.

Before she left, Cheryl told him, "RC, anything you have done God will forgive. You need only repent of your sin and of doing life your own way. Open your heart and receive Christ as your Savior and Lord."

Alone once again in his cell, RC couldn't stop thinking about Cheryl's words: "God will forgive anything you have done..." It sounded too good to be true. God would never forgive him for all the wrong he had done!

RC couldn't stop thinking about Cheryl's words: "God will forgive anything you have done." It sounded too good to be true.

Cheryl came yet again. She was concerned for RC, and felt the deep need for her children to see their father before he died. She was also anxious for an opportunity to share the good news of hope in Christ with RC.

These visits cheered RC. He loved seeing his kids. He found himself wanting what Cheryl had. He longed for her peace and joy of heart. The visits were like a breath of fresh air on a smoggy day.

Over the next year and a half at Southern State, RC continued attending AA/NA, as well as church services on Sundays with Chaplain Wilson. During the week, RC focused his attention on a lawsuit he was developing against the Camden County Jail for the way the men had been treated on the AIDS block. A paralegal friend of his, Tom, was helping him to develop a case against them. RC had an intense hatred in his heart towards the guards and administration. He was eaten up with bitterness. At times he would even dream of getting ahold of explosives to take revenge on them for the damage he felt they had done to him. The thirst for revenge that lay in his heart kept him busy at the law library. The thought of the money he could win also drove him on with a fierce passion. Even if he didn't live to enjoy the money, he would give it to his children and they would be well provided for.

Letters from Cheryl and the kids arrived regularly. These letters meant a lot to RC and he would eagerly look forward to them. On Cheryl's part, she was puzzled by RC's profession of faith in his letters. On the one hand he spoke of faith in God; but on the other, his letters were filled with his obsession with his law suit and with bitterness at wrongs he felt were done to him by the administration and others from his past. She sensed that he was powerless to forgive the wrongs done to him, and she was puzzled by the apparent absence in RC of the peace and joy usually evident in new believers.

Cheryl didn't want to doubt RC's confession of faith, but inwardly her spirit was troubled. Whenever they had opportunity to talk on the phone, Cheryl attempted to address these issues in light of Scripture. RC's confusion deepened as he contemplated his critical heart issues. He found the cost of following Christ too much – forgiving those who had offended him, forgiving those who had hurt him and those who had turned their backs on him, letting go of the revenge that lay within his heart toward the administration – it was all too much to ask!

So as not to offend Cheryl and lose this valuable friendship and connection with his children, he tried to maintain a front of Christianity. He also inwardly feared that Cheryl might be right, and deep down he trembled at the thought of standing before an awesome God who had in His hand the power of eternal life in Heaven or eternal damnation in Hell.

Cheryl prayed fervently for RC and asked her church to pray also on his behalf. She longed to see true, visible fruit in his life so she could be sure that he did indeed know the Lord.

Striving to correct his behavior and live decently, RC became a model inmate and was moved into the work release program. Shortly afterwards he was moved to a halfway house in Camden, N.J., close to the border of Philadelphia. Within the first week there, RC obtained a job working as a cook at Kentucky Fried Chicken. By this time he was also beginning to get very sick. He was suffering day and night with fever, chills, headaches and nausea. Not wanting to get sent back, he tried to hide his symptoms from the staff members. But the raging battle inside his body and the nightmare of living with AIDS had begun.

While working at KFC, he began dating the manager. He was lonely and sick, and this relationship with Gretchen offered him the needed comfort and support he longed for. He hid from her the fact that he had AIDS, fearful that she would reject him. Instead he told her that he had a liver disease. Their relationship blossomed and grew. They began to talk about moving to California after his parole.

When RC had been there close to a year, Cheryl brought the children to visit him. They spent the day at the N.J. State Aquarium and then decided to go to the Berlin Farmer's Market. RC was required to call a staff member every two hours and report his whereabouts. He wanted to take the children to meet Gretchen, but he knew this was against the rules. He called and lied about where he was. He called later and lied again about where he had been. These lies puzzled Cheryl, and she confronted him with them. The relationship with Gretchen disturbed her as well. Things were not adding up in her heart about his sincerity in following the Lord.

They stopped in at the mall for coffee before dropping him off back at the halfway house. Cheryl felt the strong burden and need to confront RC with the careless way he was handling his life. As the children strolled through the mall, RC and Cheryl talked. He disclosed to her the seriousness of his relationship with Gretchen. When Cheryl confronted him with the AIDS issue, he acknowledged that he had not told Gretchen the truth about his illness and had been sleeping with her.

When Cheryl confronted him with the AIDS issue, he acknowledged that he had not told Gretchen the truth about his illness.

Cheryl's heart was broken. Was RC a true believer in Christ as he professed or was he playing games, still deceived and headed for eternity in Hell, separated from God? She strongly doubted that RC truly knew Christ. Because he was so ill, she felt a strong sense of urgency to openly warn him lest he miss the opportunity Christ was extending to him to believe and receive Christ as Savior and Lord. Praying for courage, Cheryl confronted RC with the way of life he was leading, the lies to his authorities, the deception, his relationship with Gretchen, his rebellion, etc. Inwardly Cheryl said a prayer for courage, and then delved in.

"RC," she started, "Repentance and true believing faith in Jesus Christ always brought about a change of heart. The Bible says, *'If any man be in Christ He is a new creation. Old things are passed away and all things become new.'* When we invite Jesus Christ to reside in our lives by faith, the Holy Spirit convicts our hearts of sin, and our desire is to please God the Father and Jesus, who gave His life on our behalf. We still have a sin nature. We still can exert our own stubborn will to do wrong, but, as a good father, God will lovingly discipline us for our good to bring us back around to a biblical way of thinking and living."

Gently, yet as pointedly as she could, she warned him that the way he was living was not the way life looks when a person gives their life to Christ.

RC stared at Cheryl with piercing eyes, hating this confrontation and feeling a growing uneasiness and fear as Cheryl continued, "Don't you know, RC, that you will soon stand before the Lord to give account of yourself? You must turn from your sin and follow Christ. He is the one with whom you must set things right. He is the one in whom you must place your faith and trust. RC, you are still being deceived. You are believing that a new start with Gretchen, a new environment, a new location, will somehow turn things around for you. But as long as life is without Christ, life is without hope. The Bible says that when we "sow to our flesh we will reap destruction." Only Jesus Christ can free us from this vicious cycle. Without Christ, RC, everything *will* fall apart again."

Uncomfortable and edgy, RC shifted the conversation to safer ground. They finished their coffee and returned to the halfway house.

RC was expecting notification of his parole date to come in the mail. He was edgy as he waited to hear from the parole board. At the same time, he was getting sicker, and he was also afraid of getting out, afraid of drinking himself to death, afraid more than anything of himself! He knew the hole in his heart was still there. He knew how he had fallen every time in the past. He knew how he had let everyone down before. The nagging ache in his heart was there, the void that made him run to alcohol, drugs, crime and sex, anything to numb the ache. He just knew that he didn't have what it would take to keep him from ending up back in prison again.

So, as had been the pattern all his life, he began to again make the wrong decisions, ones that would destroy all the good that might have been in his life. He got drunk three weeks before his release. The staff members smelled the alcohol on his breath. They ordered him to his room at the halfway house. He knew this meant the van was coming to take him back to S.S.C.F.

RC was desperate not to go back to the confinement and loneliness of jail, so he climbed out the third floor window, slid down the drainpipe and escaped. Running to Gretchen's, he hid there for several weeks. Fearing he would get caught, RC and Gretchen packed their truck about 4 o'clock one morning and took off for California to live with Gretchen's relatives.

RC was desperate not to go back to jail, so he climbed out the third floor window and escaped.

When Cheryl heard of RC's escape, she was deeply upset. Not only was she concerned for RC and Gretchen, but she was thinking of RC's children, especially Rob, who seemed to identify so closely with his father. Cheryl believed that RC's salvation would be key in the healing process of the children. Out of love for her children, Cheryl earnestly prayed for RC's eyes to be truly opened. An intense burden came to her heart, compelling her to pray without ceasing for this situation.

RC and Gretchen arrived in California and lived with Gretchen's father for a few months. Within weeks of their arrival, RC became extremely sick. An intense fear of death overcame him.

42

One day as he lay sick, with his eyes fully open, he looked up to see three huge angels in white and radiant apparel, soft and glowing. They spoke all in unison with one message. "Get up!" they said. "There is work for you to do." As quickly as they had appeared, they disappeared, leaving RC shaken and confused.

At first he thought he was crazy. Then he decided it was a hallucination due to the illness. But deep down he sensed that it had truly been a message for him from God. Quickly he dismissed the thought as completely impossible.

Shaking in fear, he called Gretchen and told her what he had seen. His health improved. RC got on with his life, but could never stop thinking about the angelic messengers and wondering what had actually taken place. He felt in his heart that if it had been a real angelic message, it might just happen again! He found himself saying, "Maybe there really is a God." In his heart he longed for further proof.

Shortly after this, RC learned that Gretchen was pregnant. The news scared him to death. Although by this time he had told her he had AIDS, he feared that he had infected her. He also feared how people would respond once they found out. He was angry with himself, but more than that he was fearful. He just wanted to escape from the fear and pain.

Remembering a partying friend of Gretchen's brother, he gave him a call. They got together and spent a couple of days drinking and doing drugs. After this binge, things again settled into somewhat of a routine. RC and Gretchen had moved onto her brother's land and were helping him with his nursery and landscaping business.

RC was having good days and bad days with his illness, and still struggled to keep his alcohol in check. Finding the pain getting worse, he started drinking again to try to numb it. But the drinking gave him severe liver pain and he found himself bedridden again.

One day, while lying in bed, he looked up and at the foot of his bed he saw an angelic form, soft and glowing, but this time could not make out the facial features of this man. The man motioned with his left hand swinging outward and said, "Get up! I have work for you to do." RC was paralyzed with fear.

Holding his chest, fearing heart failure, he lay there for what seemed like hours.

Finally he called for Gretchen and told her about the visit. He told her they must go back to Pennsylvania. In his heart RC knew he needed to go back to make things right. So, they began making arrangements to sell their possessions and move back.

One day, while lying in bed, he looked up and at the foot of his bed he saw an angelic form.

A few weeks later they were back in Pennsylvania. RC moved back to his old neighborhood in Norristown. He tried to keep a low profile for fear that the police were watching Dana's house where he and Gretchen frequently hung out. The vision and word spoken to him, which he believed came from Christ, stirred his heart with an uneasiness and fear that he could not escape. He began to drink and do drugs with a vengeance, trying to escape his own confused and frightened thoughts.

What could God possibly want with an AIDS-infected, drug-addicted, alcoholic criminal? RC just couldn't understand it! Finally one evening, unsure of what to do, RC felt compelled to call Cheryl. He just knew she could help him, and he felt he could trust her.

Cheryl had not stopped praying for RC. The burden of prayer for him was still daily on her heart, a burden that could not be ignored or put aside.

Meanwhile, Cheryl was facing pressure within her home. RC's son, Rob, had been living with her. But his behavior had spiraled out of control and he had to be placed in another home with a family in Philly. When he left, Cheryl's heart broke. Loving Rob deeply, and feeling completely inadequate to steer him on a correct course in life, Cheryl threw herself with fresh urgency before God to plead with the only One able to help the situation. Rob needed his dad. His dad needed the Lord. Only God could heal this family. Only God could set the wrong things right.

Cheryl had not heard from RC since their talk in the mall over a year ago. She was worried that maybe he had gotten sicker and even, possibly, that he had died.

When RC had reached a point of desperation, he called Cheryl. When she heard his voice, her heart was overjoyed and relieved. RC, on his part, was desperate for answers and full of fear.

Cheryl told him plainly again, "RC, you need to repent. Turn from doing life your own way, and give your life to Christ. Prove your repentance by turning yourself in to the authorities. You must make things right with them and make things right with God.

RC answered with desperation in his voice, "If I turn myself in I will die in jail. It's a lonely, cold place to die. I just don't want to die in jail. I'm afraid."

Cheryl answered with concern, "RC, it's the only way to make things right. You must trust God with the outcome. Faith in God is trusting Him regardless of how bleak the circumstances look. Obey God's word, do the right thing by submitting to the authorities, and then trust Him with the outcome of your future. If you die in jail, you will be dying in the will of God and standing before Him with a clear conscience."

After their phone conversation, RC was determined to make the wrongs right. Even if he died in jail, he knew he had to turn himself in. He wanted to show his sincere repentance, his sincere desire to do right in the eyes of God and man. There was also a fear of God working in his heart stronger than a fear of dying in jail. He longed for peace with God, but was it truly possible?

He began right away to make arrangements to turn himself in. He was concerned about Gretchen and their little newborn son. RC had taken all the rent money and used it to buy drugs. The landlord was threatening to evict them. He called Cheryl again, explained the situation, and asked her if there was anything she could do to help. He gave her Gretchen's phone number. Then he contacted a relative for help; he needed someone to drive him to the police station. Unknown to RC, the police were monitoring the call.

It was late at night when RC went to a parking lot to meet

his relative. Before he knew it he was surrounded by police cars and officers. They told him to take his hands out of his pockets and put them over his head. A strong thought crossed RC's mind at this moment: *Pull out your pack of cigarettes like a weapon - they will all shoot you and your miserable life will be over.* Pushing this thought out of his mind, he slowly raised his empty hands over his head.

Part II
Turning to Christ
and Into a Disciple

Finding New Life In Christ

On April 3, 1994, at 2 a.m., RC again found himself locked up and thrown into the "hole"—solitary confinement—at Riverfront State Prison. The officer in charge ordered the mandatory urine test. It tested positive for cocaine. In the "hole" RC was stripped of his clothing and all his possessions. He was cold, confused, and very sick from his illness and all the drugs he had been taking. He felt certain that death was close.

The words Cheryl had spoken, though, rang clearly in his mind. Christ would forgive him from everything he had done. Christ loved him unconditionally. For the first time in RC's life he actually believed that this was true.

He was cold, in great pain, broken in body and spirit and crying inside as he dropped to his knees on the hard, dirty floor. "Lord," he prayed, "I don't know what you could possibly want with an AIDS-infected, drug-addicted prisoner, but I give my life to you. I am sorry for everything I have done. Please forgive me. Show me what you want me to do with my life."

Before RC was even off his knees, the peace of God, which truly passes all human understanding, flooded his heart and mind and being. He just knew everything was going to be all right.

A few days later RC was transported to Southern State Correctional Facility where he would finish out his time. There he was again placed in the "hole."

An inmate came around with a cart of reading material. He handed RC two magazines—a People magazine and a Decision magazine. RC asked for a Bible. The man located a Bible ripped in half. He handed RC the New Testament half.

In the past RC would have picked up the People magazine and thrown the other down. This time he knew his heart had changed. He pushed the People magazine aside and picked up the Decision magazine. He started to read. The Scripture verses quoted in the magazine jumped off the page. RC understood what the verses were saying! His heart leaped for joy; he understood Bible verses for the first time in his life!

RC began to drink deep of the words of the Bible, like a thirsty man finding water in the desert. Reading the New Testament night and day, he soon finished it. Having completed it for the first time, he sat on the end of his bunk in his cell and cried and cried and cried. He just knew that this book was true. This beautiful, wonderful book was not a mass con-

RC understood what the verses were saying! His heart leaped for joy.

spiracy, as he had been led to believe by his friends. It was not fables and stories told by man. It truly was the living inspired words of God! How could he have been deceived for so long? Why had it taken him so long to understand?

That day RC made a decision in his heart; he would tell as many people as he could that Christ was real and that complete forgiveness was possible through the completed work of Christ on the cross. He would let them know that the scriptures were true and applied to every generation because they were the inspired words of God, the Creator of all mankind.

But there was one obstacle to telling others the truths that had so profoundly reached into his soul: he was still in solitary confinement.

Early one morning, several weeks later, the guards banged on his cell door. They handcuffed him and made him walk backwards down the block, at the end of which was a cage. They locked him up in it. When RC turned around there were captains, lieutenants, a magistrate and guards standing around his cage.

When they finally spoke, they listed the charges: dirty urine, escape...; the list went on. They asked RC how he pleaded. Remembering the Lord, RC answered with honesty and integrity for the first time in his life. He pled guilty to all the charges.

After several minutes of discussion with a paralegal from

the prison who was representing RC, they ruled that RC's due process had been violated. They had placed him in solitary confinement and had forgotten about him. He had not been given any medications, nor had he been given a speedy trial. Therefore, all institutional charges against him had to be dropped.

RC still needed to clear up state charges. To clear these he needed to stay in jail only one year instead of the four he otherwise would have had to serve. He was taken back to his cell until the paperwork was processed, after which he would be moved into a cell with the rest of the prison population.

As he sat alone on his bunk thinking about everything that had just transpired, it hit him! This was a true miracle of the Lord! Only the Lord could have performed this unexpected change of events. He began to realize just how powerful God is!

When the guards came to transport RC to Unit 2, in his heart he was singing one of the only hymns he knew, "Amazing Grace," which he remembered from his childhood.

Before RC even entered the unit, he ran into a Christian inmate whom he knew from the past. "Guess what, Eddie, I just gave my life to the Lord while I was in solitary confinement," he called out.

"That's great, RC! Hey, look up Steve when you get to Unit 2. He's a Christian and will help you."

RC was amazed at how God was so clearly directing his first steps as a new Christian.

The guards were upset that RC had beaten the charges. To show their re-

> *"Guess what, Eddie, I just gave my heart to the Lord while I was in solitary confinement!"*

venge for what they felt was RC's getting one over on the system, they moved him into a new cell. When he was all unpacked and situated, they told him to pack up—they were moving him to another cell. They moved him three times. RC was getting more and more angry, because he knew that they were just taking out their anger on him, but he held his peace. The third time they moved him he could not believe it—what they were meaning for evil, God had turned around for his good! There was Steve, directly on the other side of RC's wall! He was so close that RC only had to lean over on his bunk to talk to this wonderful Christian man who could help him grow.

There was Steve, directly on the other side of RC's wall!

RC began to do research on his charges at the law library. Here he met Ray, who was another Christian inmate who had found the Lord as his Savior while in jail. They became good friends and began studying the Bible together, encouraging one another and praying together. How good the Lord was to provide another Christian brother and friend!

After getting out of solitary confinement, RC could not wait to get to the phone and call Cheryl to tell her of his new faith in Jesus Christ. He was a Christian and was praising the Lord with every fiber of his being for saving him.

As they talked, Cheryl was elated at the goodness of God! She had a surprise for RC, too. She had phoned Gretchen to see if there was any way she could help her out. There was an instant rapport between the two ladies, and Cheryl easily moved the conversation to spiritual things. Gretchen had a hunger and desire to know God and had been searching for the truth, for real answers.

Cheryl invited Gretchen to come for a visit. A friend drove her there. During the visit Cheryl invited Gretchen and baby Kenny to come and stay with her and her girls for a while.

Gretchen accepted Cheryl's invitation and she, along with little Kenny, came to live with Cheryl. One day, after looking into the scriptures and understanding what Christ had done for her, Gretchen confessed her sins and invited Jesus Christ to come into her life.

What RC and Gretchen found out was that they both had accepted the Lord the same weekend—it had been Easter weekend. What a joy-filled phone conversation this was!

Gretchen lived with Cheryl for over a year, grew in the Lord and began to work to unravel the problems of her past.

She reached out and shared the Lord with her ex-husband. In time, the Lord brought her back the two children she had lost years before. She and her children later moved near the Palmyra Grace Brethren Church, with the generous help of an anonymous family. This family graciously paid Gretchen's rent for a year while she got on her feet.

Back in jail, Steve was making himself available to RC on a daily basis. As a new believer, RC was full of questions and hungered to know more and more about the Bible. Together they would read and study God's Word, pray together and walk and talk about the Lord. They mutually encouraged one another in this discipling process as Steve shared from his wealth and knowledge of God's Word obtained primarily through his own personal study of God's Word and RC's hunger for this knowledge.

Then, much too soon for RC, Steve received his release notice. But God had already been working to provide another brother in the Lord to assist RC and encourage him in his walk. His name was Ray.

The code of the streets was: never trust anyone. Yet, here in jail, of all places, he had found true and trustworthy friends!

RC's friendships in jail with Ray and Steve were something new to him. Never before had he had friends he trusted, could count on to be loyal and who were always there for him. Ray loved the Lord, and together they spent many wonderful hours studying God's Word, praying and talking about the Lord.

Christianity was blowing RC's mind! The code of the streets was: never trust anyone. Yet, here in jail, of all places, since giving his life to the Lord, he had finally found true and trustworthy friends!

RC had a severe problem with anger. He could go from 0-10 in seconds, erupting in a volcanic explosion of temper that left those at the receiving end of the anger stunned. Shortly after his conversion, a man in the jail yard who was hanging out with his friends decided to make RC the brunt of a joke. When RC passed by them, they squirted him with a hose. His anger flared. Taking stock of the situation, he realized he was greatly outnumbered. In blind fury, he entered his block, pulled the fire hydrant off the wall, and made his way to go out the door to take care of the prankster.

Steve was nearby and asked him where he was going. RC angrily explained to him what happened. Steve gently instructed RC not to avenge himself. He told him as a Christian he must not live like that any more. Instead, he must pray for his enemies and bless them. Right there Steve prayed for "the enemy" in Jesus' name. RC experienced a flood of peace in his heart—an exciting, new experience that left him amazed at the power of prayer. He went to his bunk, where he continued to pray for this man.

RC was even more shocked when one Sunday this man showed up for church. RC and Steve continued praying, and before long the man gave his life to the Lord. He later became one of RC's friends. Another lesson learned: prayer is powerful indeed!

The Gifts And Calling of God

One night as RC was studying the scriptures, the Holy Spirit impressed on him a verse. It was Romans 11:29, *"The gifts and the calling of God are irrevocable."* He stared at it, pondering what it could mean.

"What is my gift?" RC wondered. In his heart, he knew he was burdened for the lost to hear the good news of the gospel. He didn't want anyone to have to wait as long as he had waited in his life to hear the gospel. The Holy Spirit gave him the confirmation in his heart that his gift was evangelism.

He had a wonderful sense of mission as this knowledge sank deeply into his heart and soul. He was gifted by God to give this most precious knowledge to others so they too could know the Lord and be eternally saved from the wrath of God.

But the second part of the verse, "the calling of God", puzzled him. What was his calling? How was he to know? For days he pondered over what "the calling of God" might be in his life.

Shortly after this, a man named Jack was placed on RC's block. Jack was in his last stages of AIDS and confined to a wheel chair. RC was confronted with a huge dilemma. On the one hand, he was burdened to help Jack. No one was stepping forward to help him. Jack's needs were so obvious to RC now that his eyes had been opened and his heart changed by the love of Christ. He longed to help Jack, but to do so would be to possibly identify himself as also being ill with the AIDS virus. No one knew RC had AIDS, and he had kept it this way intentionally. People in jail did not take kindly to people with AIDS. They looked down on, avoided and even despised AIDS inmates. The risk in RC's mind and heart was so great! If he helped Jack, people might find out he had AIDS as well. The battle raged in RC's heart as he saw Jack struggling to push himself in his wheel chair over to the medical building for his needed daily medications. He wanted to help, he longed to help, he was burdened to help—but what would people think of him?

One night as he lay pondering his dilemma, the Holy Spirit spoke strongly to his heart. He realized that all his life he had lived before the eyes of men, being concerned with what men thought of him. Now he knew he needed to break from this life-long pattern and start living to please God. He knew he had to die to himself and live for Christ, not caring about the opinions of men, or even his own reputation, any longer. Then and there he determined that he *would* help Jack.

The first thing the next morning, RC approached Jack and asked him if he needed a hand getting over to get his meds. Jack looked at RC, distrust and questioning in his eyes, but responded that he did need help and would accept RC's offer. This started a daily routine of RC pushing Jack to and from the medical building.

As their relationship grew, RC had opportunities to discuss with Jack the forgiveness and love of Christ. Jack resented these conversations and only held spite in his heart toward God for allowing him to get AIDS.

As Jack's illness progressed, he became irritable and unappreciative of RC's helping hand. His anger and bitterness at life spilled over onto RC. It was in this relationship that RC first learned the humility and love of the Lord.

His initial response was to turn away from Jack saying, "The heck with him! Let him fend for himself!" But the Holy Spirit would not allow him to do so. In the meekness of the wisdom that comes from above as described in James 3:17-18, RC continued to not only push Jack's wheelchair each day, but he cared for other needs, serving in other ways as he felt Christ would do.

In his life of drugs and alcohol, RC had never been faithful or reliable. In this relationship now as a believer he was stretched and matured. Until his release from prison, RC continued to learn to be a faithful and reliable friend to Jack.

One day as RC was pushing Jack, it hit him like a ton of bricks! He finally knew what his "calling" was from the Lord: in prison he was called to serve the sick.

A few weeks after this revelation, Prison Fellowship came

to the prison for a three-day seminar. RC was encouraged and blessed by the fellowship of the godly people who had come to minister to them. Every day of the seminar, RC felt strongly that the Lord wanted him to open up his mouth and share his testimony and also about having AIDS. He was frightened in heart, yet determined to be obedient to the Lord. On the last day he shared his full testimony.

As a result of his obedience and honesty, the Lord immediately opened doors for RC to counsel and help men in the prison who also had HIV and were scared, or knew someone who did and were worried and concerned for them. Through these contacts, RC was able to share the Lord with many lost men. Even many guards who had loved ones with HIV began seeking out RC for counsel and information.

One officer was instrumental in helping RC get into the infirmary to visit the sick and dying. Officer Rodger, whose best friend had died of AIDS, would let RC know about opportunities to help an AIDS inmate in the infirmary and would make special arrangements so RC could visit.

It was unusual for a guard to help out an inmate in this

RC was able to share the Lord with many lost men. Even many guards who had loved ones with HIV began seeking out RC for counsel and information.

way. These contacts allowed RC not only to counsel and comfort people with AIDS, but to also provide many opportunities to talk about the Lord.

Shortly after the Prison Fellowship seminar, RC was asked to speak at the yearly Christian Prison Banquet organized by the chaplain. He was asked to give his testimony. While he felt honored, he was at the same time nervous about it. He knew that most of the men on his block made arrangements to come and many of them still did not know what was wrong with him.

RC contacted Cheryl about the banquet and she made arrangements to bring her daughters, Gretchen, and little Kenny, his son, who was several months old by this time.

The night of the banquet the meeting room was packed with inmates and their families. RC shared with the audience about his life of crime, drugs, imprisonment and the void in his heart until he gave his life to Christ. He shared how Christ, in one moment of time, had filled the void that RC had tried so hard all his life to fill.

Several weeks after the banquet, RC received notice in the mail that he was scheduled for a parole hearing. He was totally shocked because he did not know he would have a hearing so soon! He immediately made an appointment with Chaplain Wilson to discuss his possible release. As he reflected on the past year of being a Christian and being in jail, a fear started to grow inside him. He had seen many professing Christian brothers get out of jail only to return days, weeks or months later. He knew he did not want to be another statistic—he wanted to get out and stay out. He wanted to continue growing in the Lord and *not* return to his old life.

He began to question his Christian friends. He asked them why they had gotten locked up again and what had been their downfall.

He began to question his Christian friends. He asked them why they had they gotten locked up again and what had been their downfall. One by one RC was hearing reoccurring themes in their responses to his questions:

1. There was not a Christian on the outside to meet them and assist them with their multitude of problems when they got out.

2. Their old friends were there inviting them to places where they were again tempted. Because no one was supporting them in doing right, it was hard to say "no".

3. Without spiritual support they would put the
   Bible down. Some fell within days! Even though
   they had maintained a close relationship with the
   Lord while in jail and vowed they'd never be back, still
   they fell when they got out.

RC was shaken by this realization. He was scared on the one hand, but on the other, he could clearly see God at work in the circumstances that were gaining him an early release. But it was still a struggle.

Within a few days, Chaplain Wilson arranged for RC to see him. As they discussed RC's fear and the dilemma of so many Christian inmates, Chaplain Wilson encouraged RC by reminding him of the church family that awaited him on the outside.

RC had already made his home plan. He had been in touch weekly with Cheryl and his children now since he had turned himself in almost a year ago. He was planning on moving to Harrisburg to be near his family.

Cheryl's church was praying for him and was following his life and growth in the Lord with interest, concern and prayer. RC had been corresponding with the pastor for several months, and Cheryl had arranged for RC to receive the weekly sermons on tape. When RC received the tapes each week, he listened with a keen spiritual interest and would share them with Ray who was also growing in the Lord.

The tapes were one thing that helped RC grow in his love for the Lord. Another effort RC made to grow was through a Bible study course for prisoners that he had

On careful scrutiny, Cheryl discovered that RC was enrolled in the study of a leading cult.

heard about from a friend. He enrolled immediately, and as he worked his way quickly through his studies, he would send his graded tests and completed study guides home for Cheryl and the kids to keep safe. After completion of each book, RC would be given a certificate. These certificates meant a lot to RC, and he would send them to Cheryl for safekeeping. Cheryl's involvement turned out to be God's protection for RC.

Once again it was clear that Satan was at work trying to pervert, in a more subtle yet real way, RC's young faith. Cheryl began reading these lessons and was shocked to find that they were making additions to the Scriptures. On careful scrutiny, she discovered that RC was enrolled in the study of a leading cult! She sent a letter to RC warning him of the dangers of adding to Scripture and the fallacy of this particular group.

When RC realized his error, he sent the books back and had a talk with Chaplain Wilson. This incident was a powerful teaching aid to both RC and Cheryl. New believers with a hunger to learn and grow are Satan's prime targets, and he delights in putting false teachings across their path. They need the protection of the church and the security of a discipleship relationship.

Another strong temptation came along during this time as RC was finalizing his plans to move to Harrisburg after his release. An old girlfriend from New Jersey began writing him. She promised him a job and an apartment if he would come and live with her there. The invitation sounded tempting to RC, but in his heart he knew

RC knew there was a church family there waiting for him after his release. This knowledge got him through the apprehension he felt.

this would turn out to be nothing more than a door leading back to his old life. After discussing the situation with a Christian friend, he knew in his heart that this would not be God's will for him. He was done with the old life and knew he loved the Lord. He wrote his friend and turned down her offer.

He had never been to Harrisburg. He was a little apprehensive, but he knew there was a church family there waiting for him after his release. This knowledge got him through the apprehension he felt. He was certain this was the way that God, his Father, had prepared for him to take. How critical it is for the church that we not be ignorant of the devices Satan puts in the path of new believers!

Cheryl's church was continuing to support RC, following his growth with concern and prayer. Knowing RC was getting out soon and planning to make their church his own, the pastor had an Infectious Disease Policy guide book drawn up. The church held a congregational meeting before RC got out to alleviate the fears some had concerning the HIV virus. The pastor wanted the adjustment for RC and the church to be a smooth one.

Discipleship: Spiritual Parenting

Realizing, through weekly calls, the magnitude of the adjustments RC would be facing, Cheryl contacted her pastor on several occasions, asking for a man from the church to disciple RC upon his release and to be there for him. The pastor, on his part, could find no such man who could disciple RC. This need for a discipler for RC was critical because when a prisoner just gets out of jail, he needs a lot of assistance getting reestablished in the community. This is all the more critical when a convict has given his life to Jesus Christ.

It is hard for a believing ex-con to understand what the Bible means when it says, "Come out from among them and be separate." and "Love not the world neither the things in the world." The help and support of a nurturing spiritual relationship in the context of the church will make all the difference for a new believer just released from prison.

Another thing ex-cons struggle with is trust. The streets teach them well not to trust any one. A Christian can help an ex-con to a far greater degree if they willingly establish an ongoing discipling relationship with the prisoner before his release. Then when the enormous pressures of adjusting to life on the outside hit, the ex-con has someone to run to for wise counsel, support, encouragement and assistance. Without a strong believer close by, the temptation to run back to his old friends and old habits can be overwhelming.

The believing ex-con often has a head full of scriptural knowledge, zeal and passion for the Lord that can add enormous life to a church, but they often have little practical understanding of how to use this knowledge in daily life.

Living on the outside would demand that RC make enormous adjustments in order to make it. He had full-blown AIDS with all the accompanying problems as well as cirrhosis of the liver and Hepatitis C. He would have no job, no place to live, a strong addictive personality from a lifetime of doing drugs, a broken relationship with his wife who was not a believer, and children he had lost touch with and was greatly concerned about. As for his financial situation, all his earthly possessions would fit in the box the jail gave him! Add to this RC's feelings of inadequacy about how exactly one lives the Christian life, and it is understandable why he held some apprehensions concerning his release.

As the day grew nearer for his parole hearing and no man stepped forward from the church to help, both RC and Cheryl found comfort in the knowledge that God was bigger than the problems ahead.

The parole panel told RC that he was being released. RC walked out in shock and with great joy in his heart, knowing that truly the Lord had work for him.

Three days before Christmas, RC went before the parole board. They asked him a few questions about his escape. RC had determined ahead of time to answer honestly. The parole panel had a little discussion and finally told RC that he was being released as soon as the paper work was received by Pennsylvania.

RC walked out in shock and with great joy in his heart, knowing that truly the Lord had work for him to do on the outside.

The Big Day

RC waited anxiously in the front area for Cheryl's arrival. They had developed a close friendship during this last year of correspondence, and RC was glad in his heart that a friend was coming to the jail to pick him up. He was looking forward to attending services at the Grace Brethren Church that evening for Wednesday night prayer group. He was excited to meet all the Christians who had been praying for him and writing him during this last year in jail.

As RC sat in the waiting area, he remembered again a verse the Lord had given him the night before in his devotions, "I will teach you and instruct you in the way you should go, I will guide you with my eye" (Psalm 32:8). This promise of the Lord had given RC joy and comfort, something to stand on as he was being released, a promise to hold on to.

He was finally done with prison and was entering life as a new believer.

When RC saw his daughter Joanne and Cheryl, his heart leaped for joy. He was finally done with prison and was entering life as a new believer with hope in God and confidence in God's Word. He determined to hold onto his Bible like a life preserver in a raging sea, knowing that God's Word alone could light his path aright. God's Word would not mislead him, and God's promises were for him to claim personally.

RC put his box of possessions in Cheryl's trunk and got into the car. Riding down the road, his heart was happy. Like Abraham he didn't know the place where he was going—only the name—but he knew that God's hand had led him, and he believed that God would take care of him.

The first stop they made was to see RC's wife and children. RC had written Dana on several occasions, explaining his new life as a Christian and his desire to repair his relationship with her. So far he had not had any success in convincing her to come back to him and live with him in Harrisburg.

When they arrived at Dana's house, he said a quick prayer in his heart and entered. Dana was glad to see him and agreed after some discussion to give things a try. RC would go on ahead and Dana would be ready in a couple weeks.

So they got back in the car rejoicing and continued on toward Harrisburg. RC was overjoyed again to see his baby son, Kenny, already a year old, and his daughter Joanne, who had been adopted by Cheryl. It was a wonderful reunion! They all headed out the door together for prayer meeting at the Palmyra Grace Brethren Church, rejoicing in the goodness of the Lord.

RC had barely entered the church when he was greeted by Leslie, one of the women of the church. She walked up to him and said, "I am so glad to finally meet you. I have been praying for you for two years." RC knew by looking in her eyes that what she said was true. Immediately he felt accepted and loved.

Next, he met the pastor and his wife, who warmly welcomed him and shook his hand. Then RC met the rest of this warm and caring congregation. As he looked into the eyes of each one, he knew he was accepted and he knew he was loved. In all his life he had never experienced this assurance.

That night RC fell asleep experiencing a new kind of "high," a high unlike any other high he had ever experienced. It was the ultimate high that comes from being loved and accepted by God's people. That next morning the sun seemed to shine brighter than RC had ever remembered it. He was feeling like a strong soldier for the Lord. A little encouragement went a long way, and RC was ready to set the world on fire for Christ!

As RC went looking for an apartment that morning, he thought to himself that no one was going to give him an apartment. He didn't have a good credit history and had never before paid rent or bills during his past life of addiction. So getting a place to live seemed impossible.

He went to an apartment on State Street with Cheryl and told the truth to the landlord showing the apartment. The landlord said he would call the next day and let RC know one way or the other whether he could live there. RC went away saying to himself that he might as well forget it—the landlord was not going to call him. Yet the very next day the phone did ring! Miracle of miracles, the man agreed to give RC the apartment, even with full knowledge of RC's past! The church chipped in and helped RC pay his first month's rent. The Lord was already moving in miraculous ways.

That first Sunday after RC's release, someone in the church asked RC what he would like to be called—RC or Bob. RC had kept his street name for years and years. In a way he was drawn to hold on to it, but a voice inside his heart spoke clearly to him, urging him to make a complete break with the past. Hesi-

From that day on, everyone knew RC as "Bob," and it was as "Bob" that he was introduced to his first church family.

tating only a moment, RC gave his answer. From that day on, everyone knew RC as "Bob," and it was as "Bob" that he was introduced to his first church family.

That first week out Bob needed to get connected to a doctor. He went to an AIDS organization in the city. Bob's caseworker was a wonderful Christian woman named Naomi. She loved the Lord with her whole heart, and she loved people. Bob could not believe how carefully God was orchestrating every detail of his new life—even down to the finest detail! How good the Lord was in directing him to this wonderful friend! She not only encouraged him in the Lord but also helped him get connected to a doctor that very week.

During one of Bob's conversations with Naomi, she told him about a needy group of people. When someone with AIDS died, their spouse and children were cut off from the program, leaving them without resources to assist them. Right there a burden was placed in Bob's heart to help these needy families. He longed to help other people suffering with AIDS, but also to help those left behind after a death. He knew in his heart that these people needed to be reached with the love of Christ.

A few days later, Bob moved into his first real apartment! The next day Dana, along with their two children, Chrissy and Nar, moved in.

They started attending church as a family. Bob longed to raise his children in the Lord. He longed to see Dana come to a saving knowledge of Jesus Christ. For several months they worked hard to make a go of it, but it soon became obvious that they were living two completely different lifestyles. A few months later, Dana left, taking the children with her. She missed her old life and wanted to get back to the way she used to live.

He knew he had put Dana through hell during his old days when he was getting drunk and high, but now that he was living correctly she wanted nothing to do with him!

Bob was devastated! He couldn't figure this out! He knew he had put Dana through hell during his old days when he was getting drunk and high, but now that he was living correctly she wanted nothing to do with him! His loss was compounded by the fact that he again lost two children with whom he had just begun reestablishing a relationship.

In confusion, pain, and frustration, with no man next to him to keep him strong, RC threw his Bible down in despair and took matters into his own hands. Returning to the old, familiar road of dealing with life's problems, RC went out and got drunk and high.

The next morning he awoke, strongly convicted in heart and so sick in body he was unable to get out of bed. Reaching over on the floor, he picked up his Bible, held it close and told the Lord he was sorry. He opened his Bible and searched the now-familiar pages for comfort and promises that he knew would not fail him.

The first Sunday back in church after he was able to get around, Bob was encouraged by the pastor to investigate fulfilling his vision of helping the needy families who were falling through the cracks after the death of a spouse with AIDS. He had longed to do something of this sort during the months that Dana lived with him, but their problems had made him incapable of pursuing this route.

Now he determined to fully devote himself to the work of this ministry—serving the Lord by reaching out a hand to the needy.

Part III
Grace House

The Prayer of Faith

It did not take long for Bob to have the opportunity to pursue his vision of helping a needy family. Within a couple of weeks, Naomi, Bob's case worker, called Bob to tell him about a family that was in need of food. The mother had just died of AIDS, leaving several children in the care of elderly grandparents.

Bob was at this time living on his meager Social Security check. He had rent and bills to pay with little left over each month. But his faith in God was growing as each moment, each day, each week he saw that God was providing for his needs and had never let him down.

He gathered what he could from his own cupboards and refrigerator and took the food to the needy family. He reminded himself of the verse in Luke 6:38 which says, *"Give, and it will be given to you: good measure, pressed down, shaken together, and running over will be put into your bosom. For with the same measure that you use, it will be measured back to you."* He knew the promises of God were his to claim.

He had given away his food with no money with which to purchase more. Now he would watch to see God prove His Word to be true. He told no one what he had done. That night he went to bed happy to have been used of God to serve others and content in his heart that he belonged to God and God would provide.

The next morning there was a knock on his door. A Christian friend was there with bags of groceries. The Lord had burdened her heart and she had brought a wonderful variety of bread and milk, cheese, fruits and vegetable and even desserts. Even though Bob had been trusting God, he was totally stunned to see God fulfill his word and promise so quickly and bountifully. From that day Bob knew and did not doubt that God would place in his hands all he needed to help others, while still blessing him besides. He believed that the "prayer of a righteous man was powerful and effective." A clean heart and prayer accomplished God's purposes and plans.

Shortly after this episode someone recommended that Bob read a biography of George Mueller. As Bob read this book, his faith in God grew and he determined to pattern his life after this wonderful man of faith.

As Bob read the life of George Mueller, his faith in God grew and he determined to pattern his life after this wonderful man of faith.

The list of families and individuals needing food began to grow. The church family, a generous, caring congregation, began to donate bags of food to help with the growing food bank. Bob used his ingenuity to develop shelves out of cinder blocks and boards to stack the growing food supply in his living room. The whole room was being taken over by food, floor to ceiling.

Naomi helped put Bob in touch with a large food distribution center. Non-profit organizations helping the needy could get large quantities of good food for little or nothing. Bob set up an appointment with one of the representatives. A lady came out and checked Bob's living room food storage area. She found it to be clean and well-organized and approved him for membership with their food distribution center. He took the required classes and set up his first appointment.

They scheduled his first visit and he went out on the appointed day. Arriving home from his first visit he picked up the phone and called Cheryl. He was so excited! The Lord had intervened in a huge way! The food distribution center was beyond belief. Bob had come home with so much food and such a wonderful variety and only costing a small amount of money.

Bob invited Cheryl on the next appointed day and they both felt like two kids in a candy store. They had such fun finding good nutritious foods, snacks, cereals, fruits and vegetables and even candy to provide for the people now using the food bank!

A Name

People were now beginning to ask Bob what the name of his facility was. He laughed to himself, because they didn't have a facility and they didn't have a name. He knew in his heart that his ministry needed a name, a name that glorified the Lord. Their pastor began praying with Bob and Cheryl about the name. After some discussion between Bob and Cheryl, they decided on Grace House.

The name was affirmed in their minds and hearts on Sunday, when they learned that their pastor had also come up with the same name. Grace House would provide a food bank for the needy and counseling services for those with addictive behaviors, as well as support and counseling for those suffering with AIDS. Little did they know that God had even bigger plans.

They decided on Grace House. This name was affirmed in their minds and hearts when they learned that their pastor had also come up with the same name.

A Room of Love

Around September of 1995, Bob began fixing up one of the two bedrooms in his apartment. He did not know for whom he was preparing the room, but the Lord was burdening his heart to take in a man afflicted with AIDS. Bob put care and love into every detail—placing a fish tank, plants, pictures, and anything else he could think of to make the room cheerful and inviting. For months, in his spare time, he devoted himself to this task. There was not much spare time, as his life was full of service for the Lord, visiting the needy, doctor's visits, spending time with his children and with Cheryl's family, and being faithfully involved with his church.

Bob wanted the room to be a haven of rest. He himself knew by this time what it was like to be bedridden. He'd had AIDS now for six years, and along with the illness came a variety of ailments. He had been experiencing crippling bouts with neuropathy a few months before Dana left. These painful spells would leave him bedridden for weeks.

Time passed, and the room Bob was preparing took on a beautiful and comforting look.

Filling the Room

Cheryl's desire to reach out to her children's parents with the message of Christ's saving power and love was a strong and continual burden placed on her heart by the Holy Spirit. In the fall of 1996, Cheryl took Joanne, Andrea, and Ann, three of her five girls, to see their mother. Cheryl invited Bob along and together they prayed for an opportunity for him to share with Susan what the Lord had done for him.

They had a wonderful visit. Susan, as always, was thrilled to see her children. Later Bob and Susan took a walk and the Lord gave him a wonderful opportunity to share Christ with her. Susan could not get over the change in "RC" and listened with interest as he told her about his conversion and what had transpired in his life since this decision.

During this visit an old friend, Linda, who lived upstairs, stopped by. She was as skinny as a rail, malnourished, high as a kite on drugs, and obviously suffering from AIDS.

On the way home Cheryl and Bob talked and talked. Their hearts were broken over Linda's condition. Bob had known Linda most of his life! It was hard for both Bob and Cheryl to realize that she was so close to death and a Christ-less eternity in hell. They determined that they would come back soon and share the Lord with her.

For weeks Bob and Cheryl prayed for Linda; the church also intervened in prayer. A couple of days before Thanksgiving they made a trip to Philadelphia to take turkeys for Thanksgiving dinner, hoping for a chance to share Christ with Linda.

Bob brought his Bible in. While Cheryl talked with Susan downstairs, Bob went upstairs to talk with Linda. Linda lived with Randy, her boyfriend, who was also the father of Ann, the youngest of Cheryl's adopted daughters. Linda and Randy ran a crack house from their apartment. When Randy answered the door and saw "RC" standing there with a big black thing tucked under his arm, he thought Bob was there to hold him up for drugs, as he might have done in his former days. Randy was relieved to discover that the black thing under Bob's arm was a Bible. Bob sat down, and opening his Bible, he looked at Randy and Linda. "I'm here to share the Lord with you," he told them.

Linda became immediately uncomfortable and left the room, going downstairs with Susan and Cheryl, who were visiting in the kitchen. Bob's heart dropped when Linda left the room. Wasn't this why he was here? Wasn't this what they had prayed for: Linda's salvation? Inwardly Bob just knew God still had a purpose.

Randy broke the silence. "I'd like to hear about the Lord," he said.

So Bob took Randy down the Roman's Road* and on to other passages of Scripture dealing with repentance of sin and believing faith in Christ as Savior. Then Bob brought Randy downstairs and Cheryl and Bob together encouraged him to follow the Lord. Right there in Susan's kitchen Randy gave his heart to the Lord, with Bob leading him in the Sinner's Prayer. The angels in heaven broke out into songs of rejoicing, and Randy's name was entered into the Lamb's Book of Life!

> **Randy broke the silence. "I'd like to hear about the Lord," he said.**

Bob and Cheryl encouraged Randy to come back to Harrisburg with them, an offer he was not ready to accept. To Randy the thought of leaving all that was familiar to him was frightening. But the Lord had His own plans for Randy.

Bob and Cheryl and the children went back to Harrisburg with hearts rejoicing in God's goodness, and yet still heavy for those they had just left.

Three weeks after Randy gave his life to Christ, Susan called Cheryl to let them know that Randy was in the Episcopal Hospital in Philadelphia, dying of pneumonia. The doctors gave him only five days to live.

Cheryl called Bob with the news. They were both devastated. They decided to go down the next day, taking Ann with them, to allow her to say goodbye to her dad. Ann had only known for a few short months that Randy was her father. She was anxious to see him one last time.

After arriving in Philadelphia, Bob, Cheryl and Ann stopped on Kensington Avenue to stretch their legs and get a bite to eat before going to the hospi-

Randy was in the Episcopal Hospital, dying of pneumonia. The doctors gave him only five days to live.

tal. A small argument started over something small and insignificant. Soon Bob and Cheryl found themselves arguing. The argument escalated into ugly words with blaming and accusations flying in anger. Cheryl took Ann's hand, and together they left the car to get away from the tension. Cheryl needed to calm down. Bob needed to get a grip.

At this point in life, Bob and Cheryl were aware of Satan's strategies, but were still naive in their awareness of how skilled Satan is at causing division in his attempts at keeping spiritual things from happening. The Lord had been working not only in Bob's heart to prepare a room for someone in the last stages of illness, but God had also been working in Randy's heart as well. Randy was a brand new baby Christian with a lifelong drug addiction. Three weeks old in the Lord, he had still been using drugs every day and was still running a crack house. The Lord had disciplined Randy in His love and mercy, landing Randy on his back in the Episcopal Hospital. What was about to occur was a divine appointment—a supernatural meeting. Satan was bound and determined to prevent this from happening, and had almost succeeded.

Bob and Cheryl were both feeling a bit raw from their fight. Finally, Cheryl walked back to the car where they were able to talk it over. God allowed them to see that they were falling into Satan's scheme to destroy God's plan for Randy. Apologies made and accepted, they continued on to the hospital, praying as they went that God would use them to comfort Randy during what they thought would be his last days on earth.

Arriving at the hospital, they went to the intensive care department. They were led by the nurse into one of the small rooms, where lay the mere shell of a man. Randy had lost a great deal of weight and was skin and bones, dehydrated and pale, weak and unable to even sit up.

His heart was happy to see the group, happy to see Ann his daughter once again, happy to see his old friend Bob who had been so visibly changed by the love and forgiveness of Christ, and happy to see Cheryl, whom he had only just begun to know. They prayed with Randy and encouraged him in the Lord.

At the end of their short time together, Bob held Randy's hand and asked him who would take care of him if he were discharged. Randy shook his head, not knowing. Bob told him he had a room ready for him and that he would take care of him. Randy started to cry and said he would go to Harrisburg to live with Bob when he was released.

Before they left, the nurse called Bob aside and told him privately that if he were to take Randy home he would need to make burial arrangements right away, as Randy would not live much longer.

Good-byes were said with tears. They left not knowing if they would see Randy again.

Two days later Bob drove back with a Christian brother from the church to pick Randy up and bring him home to his apartment on State Street in Harrisburg.

On the trip home, Bob's heart and mind were spinning. The reality of the responsibility he had just taken on had begun to settle in, but he was blessed by the knowledge that this was his opportunity to be Christ's hands and feet for Randy. What would Jesus do? How would Jesus be in this situation?

When they arrived home, Bob knew Randy needed to be bathed. There were years of who knows what embedded in his body and under his nails. Bob helped Randy get in the tub and in a labor of Christian love and brotherhood scrubbed him from head to toe.

There were many prayers sent heavenward on Bob's behalf that he would not catch pneumonia as he ministered to

Randy. Bob felt a peace and total confidence in the Lord that this was the job the Lord had given him.

Bob helped Randy get into his new pajamas and helped him into his bed under clean sheets and warm blankets.

Bob checked on Randy throughout the night, making sure he was all right. Randy was making gasping noises, rattling and wheezing.

The next morning Bob took Randy to Hershey Medical Center. After a few hours of waiting, they learned that Randy had been sent home without his proper medications. Hershey Medical Center prescribed medications for Randy and he was again sent home.

As Randy slept, Bob made arrangements with a local funeral home for his burial. But God had other plans for Randy.

A couple days later Bob lay napping in his bed in the afternoon. He awoke to the sound of water running. Rising from bed, wondering what water faucet he had left on, he was shocked to find Randy in the kitchen doing the dishes. Bob's heart leaped inside him; he just knew now that Randy was going to make it!

Randy began regaining his strength, both physical and spiritual. Now that he was in an environment where he could grow as a Christian, he really he took off! His eyesight was still very poor, being weak from his recent illness, so he was unable to read. But he was able to hear just fine, so he would sit for hours on end listening to the Bible on cassette. Every day he seemed to grow more and more in his love for and commitment to the Lord. A strong bond of Christian love and fellowship grew between Randy and Bob, and they encouraged and sharpened one another in the Lord.

Grace House Finds a New Home

As the ministry, and the list of people needing food and counseling, grew, Bob and Cheryl became aware of the need for a permanent home for Grace House. They began to discuss purchasing a house where Bob and Randy would live and still have plenty of room to run the food bank and counseling ministry, and possibly even take in others sick with the AIDS virus—a hospice of sorts.

They knew they needed wisdom and direction from the Lord and began praying together and seeking the Lord, asking the church members and other concerned believers to pray. Bob and Cheryl also began to search for other AIDS hospices and organizations in the surrounding area. They discovered three such organizations and set up appointments to see the homes and organizations to glean wisdom and insight.

After each appointment they became more convinced than ever for the need of a Christian ministry reaching out to people with AIDS in that area.

They had only discovered one other Christian AIDS organization, located over an hour away in Lancaster, Pennsylvania. It was a wonderful Christian ministry called The Gathering Place, run by a husband/wife and family team who reached out to minister to and support people with AIDS. Though not a hospice, they served the AIDS community in a practical way, being for the sick the hands and feet of Jesus.

As Bob and Cheryl rubbed shoulders with these wonderful people from The Gathering Place, they were learning a lot. As they viewed secular hospice facilities, the need for a ministry that would minister to the body, soul and spirit of AIDS people became very clear to them, and they prayed that God would open the way.

Around this time Bob met a couple in need of food and

support. The wife had AIDS; the husband did not. They had just been evicted from their apartment due to Sam's drug addiction. Bob and a Christian friend led Sam to the Lord. Barb, already a Christian, rededicated her life to the Lord. Along with their small baby, they moved in with Cheryl and her children, who were living in a large farmhouse. Barb was very sick with AIDS.

Their needs made Bob and Cheryl more convinced than ever of the need for a permanent, larger home for Grace House.

On the first day of January, with a strong nudge from the Lord, Bob and Cheryl found themselves driving up and down the streets of Harrisburg, looking at all the houses for sale, and even at abandoned buildings, trying to find one suitable for Grace House.

They had a prayer in their hearts, faith in a big God, and no money.

They wrote down some phone numbers and made some calls. That afternoon, when they arrived home, there was a message from a realtor, Dave. Unbelievably Dave was a former Catholic priest with a heart for ministry. He was not a Christian, but knew instinctively what type of location and house was needed. Even more exciting, he knew just the place! He gave them the address and told them to meet him there that afternoon.

Bob and Cheryl found themselves driving up and down the streets of Harrisburg, looking at all the houses for sale, and even at abandoned buildings, trying to find one suitable for Grace House.

Excitement was pounding in their hearts as they pulled up in front of the large, two-story red brick house situated right on the edge of the worst projects in Harrisburg. Having arrived before Dave, they took a look around. The house, though in great need of repair, was structurally sound and beautiful to their eyes and hearts. A larger-than-usual yard for a city home surrounded the house.

Without a word uttered between them, they both knew this was the place. As they began to talk with one another, the excitement and joy combined into one. Together they joined their prayers, asking God for his leading and direction in acquiring this house.

When Dave arrived, he showed them through the house. The windows were draped with blankets, giving a dark and eerie feeling to the house littered with trash and garbage. It was unfit for human habitation, yet the rooms were filled with people lying everywhere, strung out on drugs. It was obviously being used as a crack house.

The appearance of the house did not deter Bob and Cheryl from seeking the Lord's direction in acquiring the house. They both knew this was the right place. The only question in their hearts was how the Lord would provide the $10,000 purchase price for the house.

By faith they knew that God would provide. They prayed two specific requests: first, for $3,000 to put down on the house; and second, for the Lord to intervene by peaceably removing all the people in the crack house.

The people living there were all squatters, using the water and gas and electric, but not paying any rent. The landlady was losing more and

They had a prayer in their hearts, faith in a big God, and no money.

more money, since she was not receiving rent money to pay the bills. This was why the house was being sold for $10,000. She was taking a loss, and would not even be able to recover what she owed in back bills.

About a week later, Dave called Bob and Cheryl and told them to come and board the house up. Everyone was gone! Not a squatter was to be found! When they asked Dave what had happened, he told them that everyone in the house had been on probation or parole. There had been a drug bust, and everyone had been locked up.

That same day they went out and met Dave at the house to help him board it up.

But they still needed the deposit money to sign an agreement of sale. They began praying that the Lord would give them His "go ahead" by providing the $1,000 needed.

A few days later a letter came in the mail from an old friend of Cheryl's who knew nothing about what was happening. In the letter was a check for $1,000 with a note saying the Lord had put them on his heart and the money was to be used as needed! They were elated and praised the Lord again and again for His faithfulness and clear direction.

The next day they signed an agreement of sale and set a date for the closing that was to take place three weeks later, on March 12, 1996. At the closing they were required to bring $3,000. They were still trusting the Lord for the money.

They had acquired a Pontiac Grand Am that needed extensive bodywork. It was the money from the sale of this vehicle that they were going to use for settlement. The car was in the shop, and there had been delays and setbacks. It was finally finished two weeks before their closing date. They listed it in the newspaper, asking $3,000 for it.

Three days before settlement they still had no buyer. Bob, Cheryl and Randy got together and prayed, placing the need before God alone.

Within an hour after their time of prayer, the phone rang. A Christian man was looking for a car for a friend in need that he was helping. When he came out and saw the car, he immediately knew it was what he was looking for. He gave them the $3000 in cash!

Again their gratitude and thanks to God could not be contained. They were in awe at the miraculous way God worked when they followed His plan and waited for His provision and direction.

At settlement they were able to put down the full amount required and entered into an agreement of sale for $250 a month until the balance was paid off. What a joyous day as they walked out with the deed in hand!

They went over to the house to look things over and plan their first workday. They had the wonderful opportunity of meeting their neighbor, Martha. They found out she was a dear Christian woman who had been praying for years and years for Christians to move next door. Their hearts rejoiced as they realized they were an answer to her prayers. She was so relieved and rejoiced aloud when she learned Bob and Cheryl were Christians. She had been living in fear and concern over the goings on in the house. She was so thankful it would now be used to glorify God!

Bob's lease on his apartment was up in April, so they began working diligently to get the five tons of trash cleaned out of Grace House and some of the rooms fixed up so Bob and Randy could move in when their lease was up.

Saturday was the first major workday. A group of friends from the Palmyra Grace Brethren Church came to help clean out the house.

During the week Bob, Cheryl, and Randy, along with their children— Joanne, Andrea, Ann and baby Kenny—worked hard on the house to get it ready to live in.

A couple of weeks later a group from the Johnstown Grace Brethren Church came and combined their efforts with the Palmyra Grace Brethren Church and several friends. They painted most of the downstairs and a couple of the rooms upstairs.

The restoration was far from completed when Bob and Randy moved into the house in April of 1996. But the kitchen and living room and bedrooms were habitable, the electric was on, the plumbing was fixed and they had furniture. The only major thing lacking was a heating system, but there were still several months till the cold weather would come.

The work had been hard. Fortunately, the Lord had given Bob the skills needed to do a lot of the work, such as minor plumbing, minor electric, and locks. Cheryl and the girls painted and used their domestic skills to make the house a home. There was still so much to be done! The one prayer they prayed continually before the Father during this time was that this work would be done in a manner that would please the Lord, and that the ministry accomplished here would be for His glory; that their labor would not be in vain.

Bob was suffering regular bouts of illness – fevers, pain, strange illnesses that kept knocking him off his feet at every turn. He had many discouraging, bedridden days where he faced the frustration of so much to do and so little strength.

Many prayers were going up for the establishment of Grace House and for Bob's strength and health. The Lord faithfully sent help from many churches, youth groups, individuals, and friends—more numerous than can be named. The help was gladly accepted, and the work continued to move forward.

Grace House was located at 1125 S. 16th Street in Harrisburg. There was a lot of drug activity, violence and crime in the deadend across from the house. The loud music, noise and fighting would often wake Bob and Randy from a sound sleep. These evidences of great spiritual needs

The Lord faithfully sent help from many churches, youth groups, individuals, and friends—more numerous than can be named.

of the community right outside their door prompted them to pray for these people.

In the beginning the food bank was open 9–5 every day except Sunday. They gave their name to a local organization so they could get the word out that Grace House was a place people could come to for food and counseling—not just for HIV/AIDS, but to all who needed help. In time Bob, Randy, Cheryl and others who helped in Grace House started building relationships with many of the people from the neighborhood and beyond.

God was always faithful to provide for the needs of Grace House. At times the food stock in the cupboards would get low, but God faithfully provided. Often they did not know where the food was coming from, but they began to expect by faith that when the cupboards were getting low, God would somehow fill them to overflowing again. They never had to turn anyone away for lack of food. The same was true in their finances. Month after month God provided enough funds to cover all their bills so that they were faithfully paid on time. This remains true to this day.

Luke 6:38 came to life in the ministry during these early

days—as well as all future days—but during the early days their hearts were impacted not only by the power of God, but also by His faithfulness in keeping His promises: *"Give, and it will be given to you: good measure, pressed down, shaken together, and running over will be put into your bosom. For with the same measure that you use, it will be measured back to you."*

They were still working hard to fix the house. Cheryl and the girls would come over several days a week to scrub, scrape, paint, sweep and clean. It was hard, tiresome work, and no one felt at all like cooking. The very first week of the work a friend of theirs, who also ministered in the inner-city, came over with crates full of ready-made microwavable meals—sandwiches, drinks and even desserts! They were completely taken by surprise at this simple but rich blessing that God provided for them through others.

These ready-made meals were provided faithfully every week, month after month, all during the long, hard work days; so no one had to cook, and clean up was as easy as throwing away the package!

When the physical work finally slowed down after many months, this supply of ready-made foods stopped. This was just one of hundreds of ways God showed His faithfulness in meeting the exact needs of the moment, teaching them that God was watching and caring for their needs.

They began to see the need for a board of directors—godly men and women who could help oversee the work and finances and maintain the accountability of the work. God put together a team with vision and faith who have helped and encouraged them tremendously over the years.

During this time, the local newspaper asked to do a story about Grace House. They sent out a reporter. Bob spoke with her and told her up front that he did not want an article done if Christ was left out. She quickly identified herself as a Christian and assured them that the article would present the work of Grace House in a way that would clearly give glory to God for its establishment and ministry.

God was one step ahead of them – as always. Through that article many new contacts were formed with needy people –

needing not only food but also counsel and the gospel. One day they even received a call from an Englishman who was in the States and about to return to England. He had seen the article and called because he was frightened—scared to death—that he had just acquired AIDS from a one-night stand. Bob shared the Lord with him and this dear man repented of his sin, gave his life to Christ and took Jesus back with him to England!

Linda Finds Christ

During these months Randy continued to grow in the Lord and in the Word. He was a great encouragement to all the believers. But his main focus of ministry was his girlfriend, Linda, with whom he had formerly lived and run the crack house. She was still living back in Philly in their old apartment, still running a crack house, and still afraid of the gospel. But slowly her heart was opening up to Randy's words shared with her through letters and visits. Randy told her that what God had done for him, He would do for her if she trusted Him.

In June of 1996 Bob needed to go to Philly on an errand. Randy went along to see Linda. Bob dropped him off and left to run his errand. Randy had a wonderful opportunity to talk openly and honestly with Linda about the Lord and what He could do for her. By the time Bob got back, Linda was ready to give her life to the Lord. Bob went through the Roman's Road* with her, after which Linda then prayed to receive Christ as her Savior. Randy wanted her to leave the crack house immediately and go back to Harrisburg with them, but Linda had "loose ends" to tie up. So Randy and Bob reluctantly left her and returned home.

Linda, a brand new baby Christian, was still confused about many things. With a strong heroin habit that dated back many years and running what amounted to a flophouse, it was inevitable that she would fall into her normal habit of life and get high. As incongruous as it may seem, while she was shooting up each day with the other drug addicts, she would talk openly with them about Jesus, telling them that she gave her life to Christ and that they, too, should give their lives to Him!

Randy and Bob knew her predicament. Randy had a sense of urgency about getting Linda out of Philly, so he caught a bus later in the week and went back to Philly to rescue Linda.

Battling AIDS, Linda weighed about 90 lbs. Randy finally persuaded Linda to come back with him. Bob picked them up at the Harrisburg bus station and brought them to Grace House. Cheryl was there, waiting to take Linda home with her.

After introductions and some friendly discussion, Linda was told she would go to Cheryl's to stay. Looking like a scared, cornered rabbit, Linda resisted. She and Randy had been living together for seven years. She didn't even know Cheryl! She came up to Harrisburg because she wanted to be with Randy. On top of everything she was coming off a bad heroin addiction. Bob, Randy and Cheryl explained to Linda that she could not stay with Randy until they were married—it went against God's word.

Linda continued to resist. Finally, frightened and tired, she gave in and went home with Cheryl, comforted in the knowledge that tomorrow she would be back with Randy again.

Linda was a very sick woman. She found it difficult to get off the couch, let alone walk. But slowly, with a steady diet of good nutrition, and nurtured in the love and care of friends, she "de-toxed" and began to regain health, strength and weight.

Cheryl was delighted to find Linda to be an eager learner, and soon Linda was growing strong in the Lord. As Randy and Linda grew in the Lord, their hearts turned toward their children left behind in various situations in Philly.

As Randy and Linda grew in the Lord, their hearts turned toward their children left behind in various situations in Philly.

Michael was the first to come home. Bob and Randy drove back to Philly. Michael was living with friends in Kensington. Randy explained to him that he needed to get in the truck and come home to them. Michael got in and came to live at Grace House for a while, eventually moving to Cheryl's to be with his mom.

Brenda was about 6 or 7 years old. She had been living for quite a while with one of Randy's grown daughters. Much prayer went into the trip to Philly as Linda and Randy sought to regain custody of their daughter. Fearful that Missy would not give her back, they prayed and prayed.

As things were talked out, Missy saw something different in her father: he was clean, free of drugs for the first time in years and years—and Linda was, too! Missy had been resolute at first that she would not give Brenda back to Linda and Randy, fearful that it would turn out badly for the little girl. But in the end she gave in, relinquishing Brenda's care into the hands of Brenda's overjoyed parents.

What a powerful testimony to Randy and Linda of what God could do! Their hearts rejoiced all the way home in the car. It was a high like no drug could ever give—to see a big and wonderful God doing impossible things! It was more than just a blessing to the newly-united family, it also got the healing process started in this family, which until then had been completely dysfunctional.

Lessons to Learn

Work on Grace House continued. There was still much physical labor to be done. Randy was gaining his strength and health back, but had not held a job for years—except for his and Linda's crack house, which could hardly be considered a job.

Needing help, Bob had asked Randy for a hand now and then. Randy always seemed hesitant to help. One day Bob saw him leaning on a broom. He asked him what he was doing. Randy said he was trying to decide if he wanted to help or not. "Don't you know, Bob, that I get paid by welfare *not* to work?" Randy began to be stretched as a new believer as Bob taught him the verse, "if you don't work, you don't eat." (II Thess 3:10)

A big power struggle was going on inside Randy as the Holy Spirit wielded the double-edged sword of the Word in his heart. In the end Randy submitted to the Scriptures. Not long after that, he got a job working as maintenance supervisor at the mall. Not bad for a man who not long before had been told that he only had five days to live!

Although eager to get married, Linda and Randy knew they were not ready. They knew they needed to grow more in the Lord. Finally, on October 31, 1997, they were married, and everyone sensed that the Lord's timing for their marriage was perfect.

Linda, Randy and their two children, Michael and Brenda, moved into Grace House until they could save enough money to get their own apartment. They were all still attending the Palmyra GBC, located 35 minutes outside of the city. Traveling the distance to church created a great challenge to them, since neither Randy nor Linda had a driver's license, and they had no car. There were others, as well, who wished to come along.

But it seemed that everyone who was coming to the Lord or showing an interest in spiritual things did not drive! It became a standing joke among the new believers. Bob would drive a carload of people and Cheryl would drive a second carload to church every Sunday morning, Sunday evening, and Wednesday.

While Linda still lived with Cheryl, Cheryl's mid-sized Buick was filled beyond capacity every service! Cheryl prayed earnestly for the Lord to provide a larger vehicle; and Bob prayed as well. It was a good problem, but truly a problem nonetheless.

One day a dear friend of Cheryl's, at the prompting of the Holy Spirit, emptied her savings and bought Cheryl a beautiful blue-gray GMC Safari van. Cheryl was completely overwhelmed at the goodness and faithfulness of the Lord. Not only did He provide the needed transportation, but the van was so beautiful, too!

Cheryl cried all the way home after she received the van. God's provisions were so timely and bountiful!

Discipleship

Although Bob was a growing Christian, loving the Lord and desiring to please Him, he still had deeply rooted patterns of responding, or better, reacting to people, that needed to be changed. He still needed a man to disciple him, to bring scriptural truths to light in his life and encourage him.

Bob had the desire to do right, much head knowledge about what was right, but he had little practical wisdom and understanding of how to live like Christ in his response to people in everyday situations. What he needed was someone to disciple him. He committed this need to the Lord and waited.

In time the Lord brought Pastor George Traub (Hope Grace Brethren Church, Dillsburg, Pennsylvania) alongside Bob to mentor and disciple him. Pastor George, although very busy with a growing **Bob and Pastor George continue to meet every other week for accountability, encouragement and support.** church, made himself available to Bob on a weekly basis, not just to work through the deep-seated issues in Bob's life, but the daily concerns as well. These times of discipleship and accountability were critical in the process of Bob's spiritual development. What would he have done without Pastor George! Even to the date of this writing, years later, Bob and Pastor George continue to meet every other week for accountability, encouragement and support.

As Bob and Cheryl became immersed in their own experiences of discipling, they learned that people coming out of a lifetime of drug and alcohol abuse and other addictive behaviors must have a discipling process. What they need is a discipling method in many ways as rigorous as a parent/child relationship. A parent patiently puts up with the child's crying, tantrums and messes out of love for the child, with the full expectation that eventually this little one will grow up to be a mature adult. New believers, coming straight out of the inner city, with lifelong addictions, may have never seen normal, wholesome ways of dealing with the everyday problems and challenges of life. It is unrealistic to expect that they will instantly unlearn lifelong patterns of behavior. Discipling bonds like those Jesus formed with His twelve disciples, who often erred, are critical for all new believers, and doubly so for those coming out of the inner city.

It often takes years of falling and getting up for the new believer to start "getting it right." The security, love, care, and nurturing of a discipler are the keys to the maturing of the new believer.

This, of course, does not mean that the "parent" in the discipling relationship overlooks open sin or immoral behavior in the life of the new believer. It actually means the opposite. Only this kind of spiritual parent/discipler is close enough to his disciple to not only know what's going on, but to have the kind of relationship that permits him to challenge his "disciple" and for that challenge to have a positive effect.

The mature believer must exercise every level of grace, sacrifice, commitment and love to reflect Christ's love to this new babe in the Lord, confronting sin and flaws while maintaining an atmosphere of love and acceptance.

The key to a successful outcome in bringing a disciple to maturity in Christ is that he or she is committed to turning from sin and following Christ. On this point the discipler can only teach, advise, and pray. If the professing believer does not have this attitude, but instead quickly takes back the control of his or her life, the person will return to old temptations, with no ability to resist. This individual will soon be right back in the mire of sin (Matthew 13:18-23).

Grace House has seen both kinds of disciples. How painful it has been when they have helplessly had to watch a professing new believer stubbornly hold on to sin, even after admonition and rebuke, and step away from the Church and body life, returning to destructive, sinful behaviors! But even in such cases, there is hope. After again reaping the bitter fruits of sin, and as the church prays earnestly, the Holy Spirit may again bring the wanderer to repentance. The individual then needs to be welcomed back with open arms and the discipleship relationship restored.

If the Church ever hopes to minister to the needs of the inner city, she must first grasp this point on discipleship. The Church must count the cost before plunging in, lest she find herself in the middle of a high-maintenance spiritual relationship that her commitment is not prepared to sustain. Are we willing to minister among the poor and sick who may never be able to hold their own financially?

Are we willing to invest time in people who do not even know how to crawl, spiritually speaking? Are we willing to stick with them until their crawl turns into a hesitant walk, until their hesitant walk turns into the sure-footed walk of a mature believer? This may take years, but this is the very commitment that Jesus had with his twelve disciples, that Paul had with Timothy and Onesimus and others. In his dealings with the new believers in the wicked city of Corinth, Paul put it this way, "I will very gladly spend and be spent for your souls; though the more abundantly I love you, the less I am loved" (2 Corinthians 12:15). This verse also states the risk involved in working with new believers in a discipling relationship: appreciation from these new believers for whom we are laying down our lives may be small to nonexistent. In those times of painful realization, we must remember why we do what we do. We do it for Him who loved us and gave Himself for us (note Appendix B).

Winning Mom Over

It was nearing the summer of 1997 when Bob's brother Petey called to let him know that his adoptive mother, Agnes Clarkson, had had a bad fall and was in a rehabilitation center after having hip replacement surgery.

Agnes Clarkson had been living with Bob's brother and his family. Petey was in the army and was being transferred from the States to Germany, with his family going as well. They had decided that once Agnes's hip healed, she would go to a nursing home in North Carolina.

Bob had been in touch with his mother, because he wanted her to know that his life had changed. He was trying to let her know that he loved her and was there for her if she needed him.

On her part, Agnes was skeptical. She hoped that the change was real, but after all these years of knowing "RC" ... well, she just found it hard to believe that he had changed.

Bob invited her to live with him at Grace House, but she declined. Late that summer Bob, Cheryl and three of her daughters, and Kenny went to the nursing home to visit Agnes.

As soon as she saw Bob, she remarked, "Bob, you have changed—there's a glow about you." Bob took advantage of the chance then and there to tell his mother that he had given his life to Jesus Christ—he was a Christian. She said she was happy to hear he was back in church.

Their day with "Grandmom" was wonderful. They took her out to eat and talked about her life, their lives and old times. Later on in the course of the day, Bob again invited his mom to come and live with him. This time she said, "Yes"! By now she knew that there had been a genuine change in his life—she was so convinced that it was real that she was willing to stake her future on it.

They spent the next few hours helping her pack and wrapping up her business with the nursing home. Before she knew it she was loaded in the van with them, traveling to Harrisburg to live at Grace House with her once-prodigal son.

Bob got Agnes settled in the downstairs at Grace House. She had a nice apartment with a kitchen, bath, bedroom, and sewing room. She also shared a living room with Bob. They enjoyed helping each other; Grandmom became a great help with the food bank. She also cooked meals for Bob and his son, Kenny, who now lived with Bob part-time. A lot of healing was taking place between Bob and his grandmother/adoptive mother. He apologized to her for the wrongs he had done her.

One day someone asked him why he called Agnes "Grandmom" and not "Mom," since she had legally adopted him as a young boy. He couldn't think why, so he decided then and there to call her "Mom" from then on. She had always been there for him and loved him, even when he was doing wrong.

When he first called her "Mom," she was shocked! She looked at him and said, "I waited thirty- some years to hear that from you." Bob went to his mother and hugged her as both of them broke down crying. Through his tears Bob cried, "I didn't know, Mom, I didn't know!"

She looked at him and said, "I waited thirty-some years to hear that from you."

During the first few months Bob had many wonderful opportunities to talk to his mother about spiritual matters. One day as they were talking, Bob asked his mother, who was now 89 years old, "Mom, if you were to die today, would God let you into heaven?" Agnes said, "I hope so, because I tried to do good my whole life. I went to church and raised you kids in the church."

Bob knew then that his mom still did not understand the completed work of Jesus Christ on the cross. He asked her,

"How could the thief on the cross get to heaven, since he didn't have any time to do the good works to make him worthy of heaven? Jesus told him there on the cross, 'This day you will be with me in paradise.' How could that be, if it was good works that were required for salvation?"

Agnes thought about what Bob said, and it hit her like a brick. "You're right, Bobby, you're right!" she exclaimed.

Bob then had the rare joy of leading his mom through the gospel message, sharing with her verses from Romans and from Ephesians 2:8-9. Right then and there they bowed their heads together and prayed. His mother gave her life to Jesus Christ in humble repentance and child-like faith!

Years later Bob's mother passed away from a bout of pneumonia. How they missed her! But they rested their hearts in the confidence that she was with the Lord and could raise their voices in joy as they sang the old hymns she had known and loved.

Shortly after Bob's mother moved to Grace House, Bob was able to reach out to his son Rob. Rob had been living a life of rebellion, constantly getting in and out of trouble with the law. Over the past few months since he had been in touch with his dad, he saw that the changes in his father's life were real! Rob's life was a mess. He was living in Norristown and had gotten himself into deeper trouble with the law. He called his dad and asked for help. Bob told him he needed to turn himself in and make things right with the authorities. Bob told him he would be there for him, and that when Rob got out of jail, Bob wanted him to come home and live with him at Grace House.

Rob followed his father's advice. It was not long before he got out of jail and came to live at Grace House with his dad, grandmom and little brother. He and Bob were able to repair the damage done from the past and Bob sincerely apologized in tears for all the ways he had wronged Rob while he was growing up.

Meanwhile, Rob was able to find a job that he loved, and years later he, too, gave his heart and life to Jesus Christ! The Lord has since blessed him with a wonderful Christian wife and two beautiful children. Bob and Cheryl are so proud of him!

The Lord truly gave Bob back "the years which the locusts had devoured," as one of the prophets put it. Only God could take a hardened, selfish, desperate criminal and change his heart, turning it towards his children and family.

Grace House Dedication

Around this time Bob and Cheryl began to gear up for a special dedication ceremony. They wanted to dedicate Grace House to the Lord. Bob was impressed with the need of dedicating not only the house to the Lord, but each individual room as well. This house was once used for so much evil, and so much depravity took place within its walls as it was filled with drug addicts and criminals every day. It had been dark and dirty, a den of demons and darkness. Now it had been reclaimed by the kingdom of Light for the work of the gospel. They wanted God to be glorified in every room of Grace House.

Plaques were made and hung over the doors of various rooms in honor of individuals and church groups that had worked to restore them for use in the ministry.

The dedication day of Grace House was a glorious day! There were many pastors, believers from various churches, people from the projects and many new friends that joined together to dedicate Grace House to the Lord.

Plaques were made and hung over the doors of various rooms in honor of individuals and church groups that had worked to restore them for use in the ministry.

God had changed Bob's heart from a criminal heart, bent on evil and destruction, to the heart of a child of God, useful and valuable in His service. Their prayer was that He would change Grace House from a place where evil was disseminated throughout the community to a place where God's blessing would be poured out on the community. They prayed that Grace House would be a kind of lighthouse in Harrisburg, a lighthouse where the light of the gospel could shine on people desperately lost in the darkness of sin.

A Word from Bob and Cheryl

What you have read in these pages was just the beginning of the Grace House ministry, and how God used the vision of Bob, a man transformed by the love of God, to start it. Grace House continues to open its doors to anyone in need. God has even opened the way for a duplex to be acquired and restored for the purpose of discipling new believers. The ministry of Grace House extends to all the lost, not only to those with AIDS. Anyone trapped in the mire of sin will find friends waiting to love and help at Grace House. This lighthouse will continue to shine its light in Harrisburg long after we (Bob & Cheryl) are both gone. Our prayer is that the Lord will raise up workers for the bountiful harvest waiting to be brought in from inner-city Harrisburg. The need is for dedicated believers, ready to trust God to work through them to bring hope to the hopeless, and who will live by faith, trusting God to meet their needs.

If there is anyone reading this book who does not know the love, forgiveness, faithfulness and power of Christ personally, who has not experienced the true transformation that can come only through a supernatural work of the Holy Spirit, we ask you to come to Christ in prayer. Humbly repent of your sin and recognize that God sent Jesus to die in your place. Receive Christ as your Savior from sin and Lord of your life, and you will know that joy that He reserves for His children. Romans 10:9-10 says, *"If you confess with your mouth the Lord Jesus and believe in your heart that God has raised Him from the dead, you will be saved."*

If you have received Christ into your life, we encourage you to find a Bible-believing church to help you grow as a Christian, read God's Word daily and pray in faith.

Lastly, we would like to testify to the rich life God reserves for His children who walk carefully before Him. There is a constant, ever-flowing joy in obedience to the Father that can never be compared to the temporary pleasures of the sins of the flesh. It is a joy that starts deep within and wells up to fill the soul, the spirit, the mind, the being. Nothing can compare, nothing can replace it, nothing in all the world is so big and filling and glorious as the joy Christ gives to the obedient heart.

Bob and Cheryl Clarkson
(Yes, we did get married, but that's another story!)

Grace House Ministries
1125 South 16th Street
Harrisburg, PA 17104

A Life Well Lived in Christ

It has been six years since the Lord called Bob home. Bob fought the good fight, he finished the race, and he kept the faith (2 Timothy 4: 7-8).

In his final weeks of life, Bob knew the Lord was calling him and he looked joyfully with anticipation to going home. As a couple, we reflected back on Bob's life and work. We both knew and were at peace that Bob's earthly work was drawing to a close. Bob had been suffering tremendously. Although our hearts were deeply pained at our coming separation, Bob was looking forward to Heaven—to being with Jesus, his Savior and friend, and God his Father.

Bob was a man of faith (Hebrews 11:6). He believed the promises of God with a childlike faith (Mark 10:15) and he kept his eyes on Jesus (Hebrews 12:12). Although Bob was often weak, God's power was made strong in his weakness (Hebrews 11:34) and Bob was able to run his race with endurance. We saw these things daily as biblical realities in Bob's life.

It was my privilege and joy to know and love Bob as well as serving the Lord with him in helping to establish Grace House. Grace House continues to be a lighthouse in Harrisburg, PA. The operation of Grace House has passed from Bob's direction to the capable hands of Mr. John Feldhausen, who continues to serve the Lord there with many wonderful volunteers.

Cheryl Clarkson
January 2010

Greetings in the Name of our Lord,

Grace House Ministries is celebrating the second printing of *Time and Time Again.* The second printing is significant in several ways. Foremost are the hearts and minds that have been opened to the salvation message of Jesus Christ. Additionally, the need for a second printing demonstrates the enduring nature of this ministry.

The mission of Grace House Ministries is to "demonstrate the love and compassion of Jesus Christ." The goal of this mission is the eternal salvation which Jesus Christ offers. Since its beginnings in the 1990's, Grace House has been blessed by our Lord, and His work continues in the community today. The foundation of this ministry, as described in *Time and Time Again,* is a solid biblical approach toward ministry growth.

Grace House Ministries continues advancing our Lord's work by serving over 250 families a month with programs such as a self-choice food pantry, a clothing closet, a summer program for children of the Hall Manor area of Harrisburg, a prison outreach, and various social services. We have also joined partnerships with the Central Pennsylvania Food Bank, Dauphin County Prison System, Harrisburg School District, United Way, and other agencies. The Lord truly blesses us with a group of loving, dedicated volunteers.

Most importantly, Grace House Ministries continues to spread the salvation message of Jesus Christ! If you are unfamiliar with the salvation message, please look up John 3:16 in your Bible. If you do not have a Bible, please contact us at PO Box 29, Grantham, PA 17027. We will gladly send you one at no cost.

In the service of our Lord,

John J. Feldhausen
Director, Grace House Ministries
May 2010

The Fields Are White

The fields are white;
the workers are few,
hear His voice calling you.

The fields are white;
the work is great.
Don't you know the hour is late?

The fields are white,
but God is hearing.
Are you broken, contrite, kneeling?

The fields are white,
the harvest great.
A people lost, the hour is late.

Before heaven we humbly wait.

by Cheryl Clarkson

"Cheese!" RC as a young boy.

RC and his brother

Above: RC with daughters Joanne and Chrissy.

Below: RC with son Rob, deep-sea fishing on the Miss Chris fleet in New Jersey.

Cheryl and her adopted children—all siblings.

RC, on a day pass out of jail, with Rob and Joanne at the New Jersey Aquarium.

Chaplain Wilson and Bob.

111

A family re-united—Bob's first week out of jail.

Bob with "Mom" Clarkson.

Baby Kenny, Bob and Andrea at GBC church picnic

Grace House

Top: What a mess! Above: Jason Rissler and others from the Harrisburg Discipleship Center have been helping out for years and are dear to our hearts. Below: One of the first volunteer groups, from a GBC in Johnstown.

Top: "Anybody hungry?"

Upper right: Bob handing out sandwiches and coats in Kensington.

Center left: "Give and it will be given to you"—there was always food for those in need.

Right: Father and son sharing in the work.

Dedication Day at Grace House: Bob and Pastor George Traub

Above: Bob with Luis, who is now home with the Lord.

A new believer sharing God's love

115

Above left: Cheryl with Kenny and her father, Pastor Bill Tweeddale. What would we have done without my parents' support?

Above right: Andrea is Grace House's Number One helper!

Below: Pastor Dan Eshelman baptizes a new believer from Grace House.

Above: His, mine and ours: Ann, Kenny, Joanne, Andrea

Right: Bob's two little boys, Kenny and Nar

Below: Mr. and Mrs. Robert J. Clarkson! February 13, 1998

117

Appendix A

The Anointing

AIDS is a hideous infirmity that robs health and strength and keeps its victims in constant pain and discomfort, every day, sometimes all day long. It often drags its victims to the brink of death only to release its grip—if only until the next time. All AIDS-infected people are aware that, barring a miracle, one day the virus will not release them; they will not return—they will die.

Bob suffers not only from a full-blown AIDS virus infection but also from cirrhosis of the liver and Hepatitis C. He lives in continual pain, both from the disease and from the side effects from the toxicities of the powerful drugs he has to take to keep him alive. Bob suffers daily from fevers, severe pain, declining strength and, as he puts it, the feeling that "life is being squeezed out of him."

Shortly after Bob was released from prison and moved to Harrisburg, he had a major turn for the worse. Cheryl encouraged him to look at some verses in James and see what he thought. Bob read, "Is anyone among you sick? Let him call for the elders of the church, and let them pray over him, anointing him with oil in the name of the Lord. And the prayer of faith will save the sick, and the Lord will raise him up. And if he has committed sins, he will be forgiven." (James 5:14-15)

Encouraged in heart, Bob called for the elders of the church and asked for prayer and anointing. It might be that God would choose to heal him.

Bob knew God could heal him if He desired to. His heart was encouraged, as he called for the elders for anointing and prayer.

The elders anointed Bob and prayed for God's intervention in Bob's health and for God's healing.

Bob felt the Lord's power at work through this time of prayer and anointing. The Lord did not choose to miraculously heal Bob at that time, but we saw the Lord give knew direction and wisdom in understanding how the body's immune system functioned. We were able to begin a juicing, vitamin and cleansing regime that gave renewed health and strength to Bob's body.

Bob had also been experiencing crippling effects from painful peripheral neuropathy in his feet and legs. We saw the Lord bring relief from this pain as well, allowing Bob to again walk without the aid of a cane or wheelchair, both of which had been required before.

Six years later this pain returned in full force, but God brought years of relief in which Bob was able to get around in service to the Lord.

Four times over the last seven years Bob has called for the elders' anointing, and each time we have seen the Lord raise Bob up again for continued service. And though to this date complete healing has not come, Bob's doctors are unable to explain, by looking at Bob's body and reading the medical tests they run, how Bob is even alive!

Did full healing not come because Bob lacked faith, or is it that God's arm is "too short" to help? No! Bob is convinced that, if God has not chosen to bring total healing, it is because His purpose includes using his illness in "working all things together for the [highest] good" (Romans 8:28 and 2 Corinthians 5:1-10). Bob is even able to give thanks for his illness, because he knows that, had it not been for his contracting AIDS, he never would have yielded his proud heart to God's saving grace. So Bob lives in thankfulness to God for the affliction that brought him to his knees.

Each time Bob has called for the elders of the church to anoint him, he had been facing a very bleak outlook in his health. Two different times his HIV viral load was out of control, nearing one million (which, for an AIDS patient is like being handed a death sentence). Both times, after Bob was anointed and prayed for, God intervened in bringing the viral load down. They saw the Lord give Bob's doctor wisdom in prescribing just the right cocktail of drugs available to help. Just when Bob has reached the last drug left to try, right when his present drug is no longer able to help him, another new drug becomes available. Bob has lived for years with the knowledge that he is on his "last drug," that there are "no more drugs left to try."

Yes, the powerful effect of anointing and the prayers of God's people have been felt and are part of what sustains Bob through another day, in defiance of all the rules of science and medicine.

Bob and Cheryl say, "We would encourage anyone to read James chapter 5, with full confidence and faith, and ask for the Lord's intervention, help and healing through anointing. We know that Bob is alive today—13 years after having been diagnosed with AIDS and 20 years living with Hepatitis C and cirrhosis of the liver—because of God's supernatural sustaining of his body.

Appendix B

Living by Christ's Example

In following Christ's example, we must allow for a love so great to develop in our hearts toward our new believing brother or sister that:

- •Our hearts are burdened to tears (2 Corinthians 2:4)
- •We are able to feel their weakness (2 Corinthians 11:29)
- •We mourn over their sins (2 Corinthians 12:21)
- •We labor as with birth pains, until Christ is formed in them (Galatians 4:19)
- •Death is working in us, that life may work in others (2 Corinthians 4:10-12)

We have been given—each and every one of us who believe in Jesus Christ—a sober and wondrous obligation and duty by the Lord to "*Go therefore and make disciples of all nations, baptizing them in the name of the Fahter, and of the Son and of the Holy Spirit, teaching them to observe all things that I have commanded you; and lo I am with you always, even to the end of the age.*" Amen*

The Bible doesn't say wait until we are perfect Christians and then "Go and make disciples." If we wait until perfection, we will be waiting until the coming of the Lord or until death (1 Corinthians 15:52). In writing this we (Bob and Cheryl) are deeply moved in our remembrance of God's abundant grace in our own lives personally. We know our hearts, we know that we are prone to sin, we know that we struggle daily with our sin natures and with sins that so easily ensnare us (Hebrews 12:1). We know and are so aware of our weakness; we know

and are aware of the times all too often that we have dishon-
ored the Lord by hearts full of pride, complaint, stubborness,
unforgiveness, selfishness, faithlessness, greed, anger, etc. We
look back in our Christian lives where we thought we were
smart enough to stand, but we fell (1 Corinthians 10:12). We
bow our heads before the Lord and look at the cross in humble
praise, but also true amazement that God still used our lives and
will continue to use our lives as we yield them up to Him in
humble repentance and faith. This treasure given to us by God,
the light of the knowledge of the glory of God in the face of
Jesus Christ (2 Corinthians 4:6-7), shines out of our hearts *from
earthen vessels,* and will until the day that "this corruptible
must put on incorruption, and this mortal must put on
immortality...and death is swallowed up in victory."

Bob was out of jail less than six months—a Christian for
only a year and a half—when Randy came to live with him at
Grace House. As Bob discipled Randy, Bob grew himself. As
Bob helped Randy find scriptures for the problems and situations in his life, he found new insight and wisdom in applying
those same scriptures in his own life. A Christian does not have
to wait until "maturity" to begin discipling another; it's simply
applying ourselves to the study of the scriptures and taking
what we have learned and are yet learning to a fellow believer
in a committed relationship, helping them to learn to apply
the scriptures to the problems and circumstances of their lives.

May we be men and women who look each day into the
scriptures—the perfect law of liberty and *continue in it*—not
fogetting what we read, but being doers of the work and as in
James 1:23-25 and John 14:23-24, growing in Christ-likeness
and obedience. May we learn and understand the secret of
fruitfulness (John 15:4-5). May we each arise in humility to
accept our commission, our duty and our obligation given to us
by the King of Kings and Lord of Lords—to "Go therefore and
make disciples of all nations" (Matthew 28:18-20).

Appendix C

Defeating The Enemy

Although Bob had been a believer in Jesus Christ, attended church faithfully, and was in the Scriptures daily, there were powerful forces waging what felt like daily wars inside of him.

Any time Bob faced a problem, no matter how small, any time he faced an obstacle, no matter how minute, any time he faced even normal-proportioned frustrations or discouragements, he would find himself in an enormous battle over who would run his life. The temptation to return to his former patterns of behavior and coping mechanisms—drowning them in alcohol and drugs—was at times almost overwhelming.

The impulse to run back to his old life and habits was strong, beating in his brain like a drum. Bob often heard a voice in his head, over and over again, telling him to run back to Philly, to get away and get high so the problem would go away.

Bob knew God loved him. Since he had found new life in Jesus Christ, the desire to live in the world was gone, and he sincerely wanted to follow Christ. Why then was he so powerfully tempted? Why were these voices in his head so persistent in their attempts to get him to return to his former ways? Bob and Cheryl began to search for the answer to these questions, seeking the Lord's wisdom and direction for help and guidance.

There is a controversy in the Church over whether a believer can be "demonized"—meaning that demons can reside in the soul of the believer, seeking control in areas of the will, mind and emotions. There is no question that Christ dwells alone in the spirit of the believer. Neither Satan nor demons can dwell in the spirit of the believer. But if demons are inhabiting a believer and are not dealt with through fasting and prayer, and deliverance and counseling, we have strongly come to believe and understand, by experience based upon scriptural truths, that they will continue to reside in the soul (area governing will, mind, emotions) of the believer, seeking ways to destroy his life and keep him in bondage to sin.

In time we had to face the fact that the reality Bob was experiencing in his Christian walk was not meshing with the standard theology we believed on this subject. As we returned to study again the Scriptures, we found, to our surprise, that today's standard theology on demons and their influence on believers doesn't even mesh well with what is described in the Gospels! While it is for each believer to seek out his or her position on this subject, Bob's experience is described here because we have seen that Bob's deliverance from evil forces at work in him was key to his growing to maturity in Christ.

In answer to prayer, we were put in touch with a wonderful, elderly pastor. After our first phone conversation with this man, we were so relieved to have found someone who understood Bob's situation and knew how to help them! Pastor Herritt had a deliverance ministry and served out of his home, along with his dear wife.

A week later Bob met with Pastor Herritt, a humble, godly man, well versed in the Scriptures and fearless in confronting the enemy. He spent an entire day with Bob, recruiting Cheryl to stay with them to pray during the session.

The first few hours were spent explaining from the Scriptures the position of the believer in Christ, the promises of God and our authority as believers over Satan and demonic forces.

Next, Pastor Herritt delved into Bob's past, showing Bob that many things he had thought were normal, innocent fun had evil repercussions, repercussions that he was still feeling to that day.

Finally, Pastor Herritt started confronting many demons that were making themselves known through Bob, some of whom had come into his life, handed down from one generation to another as far back as the 1700's. Each demon was confronted by Pastor Herritt and cast out of Bob's life.

Bob left with a *great* burden lifted, a new freedom from bondage, and greater spiritual strength in his inner man.

There is much more we could say on this topic, but there are many good books on this subject. We would recommend such as: *Demonization* by C. Fred Dickason, *The Adversary* by Mark Bubeck, *Defeating Dark Angels* by Charles Kraft, and *The Bondage Breaker* and *Victory Over Darkness* by Neil Anderson.

Appendix D

Not-So-Friendly Fire

When people come to Christ and commit themselves to serving the Lord, Satan unleashes a vast arsenal of firepower to stop spiritual growth and discourage the new believer in his walk with Christ. In Ephesians 6:1-9, believers are encouraged to take up the full armor of God that "we might be able to withstand in the evil day."

No one is a more vulnerable target to the enemy than the believer who takes a bold step into the light. Here in the light he is an easy target for Satan's fiery darts.

Sadly, the family of God—the very ones who are supposed to be fighting in the "Lord's Army" often become Satan's prize weapons, being used by him to inflict cowardly but deep gashes in the heart of the one under attack. First Corinthians 4:5 addresses this problem and gives the admonition: *"Therefore judge nothing before the time, until the Lord comes, who will bring to light the hidden things of darkness and reveal the counsels of the hearts; and then each one's praise will come from God."*

Many a worker has been beaten down in his spirit by the heartless attacks of his brothers and sisters in Christ—unjust accusations, whispered suspicions, false rumors, back-biting, motives called into question and every action evaluated. Even Jesus was not immune to such Satanic attacks through not-so-friendly fire. Just when the servant of God is in need of a word of encouragement and the prayers of the Body of Christ, sometimes what they're met with instead is a huge dose of discouragement.

Because the phenomenon of not-so-friendly fire is so common in the church, the following suggestions are offered here to give believers healthier ways to deal with their questions concerning a servant of Christ:

1. **Pray** for and support those in service to the Lord.

2. When a servant of the Lord is accused and it seems that there are just grounds for the accusation, bring the matter into the light. Bring it to the attention of the person being accused, so that they may deal with the accusation by either bringing light and truth to the accusation or repenting of the wrong.

3. Don't spread a rumor. This only hurts the believer further, jeopardizing the work of God, and perhaps destroying the worker's reputation to a point where it may never be fully restored.

4. Remember that we are commanded to "encourage one another daily, and so much the more as you see the day approaching." People in ministry face many discouragements in working with and serving the people God has called them to serve. They need encouragement!

5. Be a team player God can count on to maintain "the spirit of unity in the bonds of peace." We are called every day to be a living answer to Jesus' prayer in John 17:21 that believers will be one as Jesus and the Father are One, "so that the world may believe that You sent Me." Unity is therefore essential in order for revival to come.

Appendix E

The Roman's Road

The Romans Road is a series of verses ~ all from the book of Romans in the Bible ~ which explain the Gospel.

Who is good?
   Romans 3:10 ~ "As is written, there is no one righteous, not even one."

Who has sinned?
   Romans 3:23 ~ "For all have sinned, and fall short of the glory of God."

There is an eternal cost for sin.
   Romans 6:23a ~ "For the wages of sin is death."

Nothing you can do can save you.
   Romans 3:20a ~ "Therefore by the deeds of the law no flesh will be justified in His sight."

God's love has made a way!
   Romans 5:8-9 ~ "But God demonstrated His own love toward us, in that while we were still sinners, Christ died for us. Much more then, having now been justified by His blood, we shall be saved from wrath through Him."

You must place your complete faith in Jesus Christ.
   Romans 10:9 ~ "That if you confess with your mouth that Jesus is Lord, and believe in your heart that God raised Him from the dead, You will be saved."

If you really believe that Jesus Christ alone can save you ... then pray and ask Him.
   Romans 10:13 ~ "For whoever calls on the name of the Lord shall be saved."